AF480204

How to Focus on Quality Research

AMALENDU BHUNIA

Dedication

"To my beloved daughter,

In you, I see the embodiment of curiosity, determination, and brilliance. This book is dedicated to you, my inspiration and motivation, as you navigate the intricate pathways of learning and discovery. May its wisdom guide you in your own pursuit of knowledge, and may it illuminate the way as you embark on your journey of quality research.

With all my love,

[Amalendu Bhunia]"

Contents

Preface

In the rapidly evolving background of academic research, the quest of quality is the foundation upon which development is built. This book is an examination of the principles, practices and viewpoints that strengthen the persistent quest for excellence in scholarly endeavours.

In an era marked by the surge of information and the continual flow of data, the significance of perceptive, impactful research cannot be overstated. This book aims to serve as a guiding beacon for researchers, academics and aspiring scholars navigating the complex background of contemporary research methodologies and best practices.

We start by delving into the very essence of quality research, dissecting its components and unscrambling the dynamics that set outstanding research apart from the ordinary. The journey takes us through the intricacies of formulating research questions, designing robust methodologies and using analytical tools that stand the test of examination.

The significance of ethical considerations in research cannot be overstressed and this book dedicates sufficient space to talk about the moral compass that should guide every researcher. From the responsible conduct of research to the ethical implications of data collection and dissemination, we explore the ethical aspects that accompany the quest of knowledge.

As technology continues to reshape the research background, we navigate the challenges and opportunities presented by the digital age. From leveraging big data analytics to embracing innovative research tools, we explore how technology can be harnessed to enhance the quality and impact of research.

Collaboration and interdisciplinary approaches are increasingly becoming very important features of contemporary research. We argue how fostering collaboration across disciplines can lead to richer, more nuanced viewpoints and penetrate that go beyond traditional boundaries.

This book is not just a theoretical discussion on quality research; it is a practical guide that offers insights from experienced researchers, case studies from different fields and hands-on tips to raise the quality of the research endeavours.

In the spirit of continuous development, this book is an invitation to join a community of scholars committed to advancing knowledge with integrity, rigor and purpose. As we embark on the research journey or seek to improve the current practices, may this book be a trusted cohort, giving guidance and inspiration to elevate the research to new heights.

Amalendu Bhunia

Acknowledgments

The creation of the book has been a collaborative effort and it is with gratitude and appreciation that we extend our acknowledgments to those who have contributed to its realization.

First and foremost, we express our deepest gratitude to the researchers and scholars whose work serves as the foundation for this book. Their dedication to advancing knowledge and commitment to quality research have inspired the content within these pages.

To our colleagues and peers who big-heartedly shared their insights and experiences, we extend heartfelt thanks. The perspectives have enriched the discussions and provided valuable real-world context for the principles discussed in this book.

A special appreciation goes to the editorial and publishing teams who worked diligently to bring this book to fruition. The expertise, attention to detail and commitment to excellence have been instrumental in shaping the final product.

We are grateful for the support and encouragement from our institutions, mentors and the broader academic community. My belief in the importance of quality research has motivated us throughout the writing process.

To our families and friends, who provided unwavering support and understanding during the long hours of research and writing, we extend our deepest thanks. Their encouragement has been a source of strength.

Lastly, we express our gratitude to the readers of this book. It is our sincere hope that the insights and guidance presented here contribute to the enhancement of research practices and the quest of quality in academic endeavours.

In the spirit of collaboration and shared knowledge, we dedicate this book to all those who strive for excellence in research.

Amalendu Bhunia

Introduction

In the bustling landscape of academia and professional research, the pursuit of quality stands as an unwavering beacon guiding scholars and practitioners alike. Welcome to "How to Focus on Quality Research," a comprehensive guide crafted to navigate the labyrinth of research methodologies, refine the art of inquiry, and elevate the standards of scholarly output.

In an era marked by an abundance of information and the rapid pace of technological advancement, the quest for quality in research has never been more pressing—or more challenging. As the boundaries of knowledge expand, so too do the complexities inherent in conducting meaningful and impactful research. Yet, amidst this vast expanse of data and discourse, the essence of quality remains steadfast—a commitment to rigorous inquiry, robust methodologies, and ethical practice.

This book is designed as a compass, offering clarity amidst the myriad choices and considerations that accompany the research process. Whether you are a seasoned academic, a budding scholar, or a practitioner in the field, the principles outlined within these pages will serve as a roadmap for cultivating excellence in your research endeavors.

Throughout this journey, we will explore the fundamental pillars of quality research: from the formulation of research questions and the design of methodologies, to the collection and analysis of data, and finally, to the dissemination of findings. Drawing upon insights from diverse disciplines and methodologies, we will uncover the strategies and best practices that underpin high-quality research across domains.

Moreover, we will confront the myriad challenges and pitfalls that researchers encounter along the way, from biases and limitations to the ever-present specter of replication crises. Through thoughtful reflection and practical guidance, we will empower you to navigate these obstacles with confidence and integrity, ensuring that your research stands as a testament to the highest standards of excellence.

But quality in research is not merely a matter of methodological rigor—it is also a reflection of the values and ethos that underpin the scholarly enterprise. As such, we will also explore the ethical dimensions of research, grappling with questions of integrity, transparency, and the responsible conduct of inquiry in an ever-evolving landscape.

At its core, "How to Focus on Quality Research" is a call to action—a call to elevate the standards of research practice, to push the boundaries of knowledge, and to make a meaningful impact on the world around us. Whether your interests lie in the natural sciences, social sciences, humanities, or beyond, the principles and insights contained within these pages are universal, transcending disciplinary boundaries to illuminate the path toward excellence in research.

So, as we embark on this journey together, let us embrace the challenge of quality research with open minds and steadfast determination. May this book serve as a guiding light, illuminating the path toward excellence and inspiring generations of scholars and practitioners to pursue knowledge with passion, integrity, and purpose.

1. Writing the Research Paper – Quick Look

1.1 Introduction

Research is a process that entails gathering and analyzing information, generating new knowledge, and contributing to the existing body of understanding within an exacting field. Focus on research usually talks about the act of directing one's attention, endeavor, and resources toward the methodical investigation and investigation of an exact topic or question. The focus on research can be explained as (a) the researcher has to select a particular area or question to study. The topic should be well-defined, relevant to your field of interest, and able to generate significant contributions, (b) before delving into the research, it is important to review existing literature related to the selected topic. This helps to understand what has already been studied, identify gaps in knowledge, and refine your research question.

Researchers formulate research questions or hypotheses based on the literature review and understanding of the topic. These are precise statements that the research aims to address. Then research design entails planning the methodology that where researcher will use to collect data and answer your research questions. It includes decisions about data sources, collection of data, and data interpretation. In the data collection stage, the researcher collects pertinent data in line with the selected methodology. A cautious mind to data quality and reliability is necessary to ensure the validity of the research findings. After collecting the data, the researcher analyzes it based on the character of the research using suitable statistical or qualitative methods. The objective is to portray significant conclusions and answer the research questions. After analyzing the data, the researcher interprets the results from the perspective of the research questions or hypotheses. This entails discussing what the data suggests, its implications, and how it contributes to the existing framework. Based on the analysis and interpretation, the researcher concludes the research questions and highlights the significance of the findings and their potential impact on the field. The researcher discusses the broader implications of the study including how it adds to the understanding of the field, any limitations or constraints, and potential applications of the research findings. If the research is of high quality and contributes extensively to the field, it may be suitable to publish the research findings in academic journals, conferences, or other platforms and sharing the particular research sets aside others to build upon his/her research work and promote collaboration and advancement in the field. Finally, researchers regularly refine their questions, conduct further investigations, and adapt their approaches based on new information and insights.

1.2 Selecting a Research Area or Topic

Consider the individual interests, enthusiasms, and inquisitiveness. What subjects or questions attract researchers the most? Research is a long-term dedication, thus selecting a topic that legitimately connects researchers will make the procedure more agreeable and pleasing.

Conduct a comprehensive literature review on the subject the researcher is interested in. This will help to understand what has already been studied, identify gaps in knowledge, and identify areas where the research could contribute something new.

Narrow down the focus considering exact features that manoeuvre the researcher. The more particular the focus, the more convenient and realistic the research will be.

Consider the relevance and significance of prospective research topics. Is the topic pertinent to contemporary issues, arguments, or developments in the particular field? Will the research talk to gaps in knowledge or add to solving real-world problems?

Think about the feasibility of researching an exacting topic. Does the researcher have access to the required resources, data, and expertise to carry out research in that area?

If it is acceptable to build upon existing research, endeavor to take a new outlook, a novel approach, or novel insights to the desk.

Talk about the ideas with guides, professors, or peers who have know-how in the field. They can give precious advice, put forward perfections, and assist in refining the research question.

Think about how the selected research area adjusts to academic or professional purposes. Will this research facilitate gaining appropriate skills, moving forward in academic standing, or contributing to the required professional path?

Think about conducting a pilot study which can help to assess the feasibility of the particular research, identify possible challenges, and refine the research design.

Research can be hard and need lots of effort, thus the enthusiasm and motivation of a researcher will be important in nourishing the interest and commitment over time.

Consider that the research direction might progress as researchers investigate deeper into the topic. Be open to regulating the focus based on novel insights and findings.

When a researcher is unsure, it is acceptable to begin with a minor research assignment before embarking on a well-built, more striving one. This can facilitate building confidence and understanding in the research process.

1.3 Reviewing Existing Literature

Delineate the scope of the literature review and choose the particular research area or topic the researcher wants to explore. This will facilitate to focus of the search and stop information excess.

Come up with keywords and phrases that are pertinent to the research area. These keywords will be exercised to search for related literature in databases and search engines.

Begin with trustworthy academic databases, libraries, and online repositories.

Utilize the selected keywords to search for related literature. Unite various keywords and employ AND, OR, NOT to purify the search. Maintain the actual path of the search terms to use and the sources to explore.

Review the titles and abstracts of the search results to identify research papers that appear pertinent to the research. This primary screening will facilitate the selection.

Utilize reference management software to organize and store the collected papers. These tools can also help to manage citations, take notes, and make references.

When understanding the full articles, read vigorously and capture detailed notes. Identify main findings, methodologies used, gaps in knowledge, and areas of conformity or difference among authors.

Analyze the obtained literature for trends, patterns, and recurring themes. Make a note of areas where there seems to be agreement and areas where there are arguments or gaps.

Researcher identifies appropriate studies, cite them in their notes, and think about how they might add to the research or inform their methodology.

Concentrate on references within the papers that are reading and these references can lead to other related works that researcher might have missed in their preliminary search.

After reviewing numerous sources, combine the information that the researchers have collected. Think about summing up tables, concept maps, or literature review sections that emphasize the main findings, methodologies, and gaps in the existing literature.

The researcher reviews the literature and identifies gaps in knowledge or areas where further research is required. These gaps can turn out to be the basis for the research questions or hypotheses.

Literature is endlessly growing. That is why; stay updated with innovative publications and includes them in the review as the research progresses.

1.4 Formulation of a Research Question

Identify the common research area or topic the researcher is interested in. This could be based on the literature review or individual interests.

Confine the focus within the common area and think about unambiguous aspects, variables, or dimensions that the researcher finds mainly fascinating or essential.

Different research types need diverse types of questions. Identify the purpose of the research and shape the question accordingly.

Frame the research question using clear and actionable language. Avoid vague terms and ensure that the research question is exact enough to guide the study.

Confirm that the research question is feasible given the available resources and expertise. A very ambitious question might bring about challenges during the research process.

Make sure that the question is unbiased and doesn't assume an answer. This helps maintain the integrity of the research.

The research question should address a related issue or gap in the literature. It should also have the potential to contribute new knowledge to the field.

Make sure that the question can be answered through empirical research. It should be something that can be studied and analyzed.

Consider the background to which the research question will be applied. How does it fit within the broader field of study and how might it shock real-world situations?

Consider "Who, What, Where, When, Why, and How" to structure the question. These question words help to cover diverse dimensions of the research.

Formulate the research question clearly and concisely. Keep refining and rephrasing it until it precisely reveals the research goals.

Ensure that the research question is clear and specific. If someone new to the work can understand the question, researchers are on the correct path.

Avoid multifaceted questions or questions that cover too much argument. Each research question should have a single and focused reason.

Example: Investigating the Relationship between Social Media Usage and Mental Health of Students

Research question: Start with a broad question that confines the major topic of interest as 'Is the association between social media usage and the mental health of students significant?'

Break the broad question into exact variables of interest as 'How does the occurrence and extent of social media usage connect to the mental health effects of college students?' State the type of association that is concerned as 'Is the impact of important social media usage on the occurrence of anxiety and depression indications among college students significant?' State the population that is studying as 'How does social media usage influence the mental happiness of undergraduate students in a particular college?' If related, include factors that might moderate or mediate the association as 'To what extent does the level of social support from friends and family moderate the association between social media usage and mental health effects in college students?' Make sure that the questions are patent and that the variables are quantifiable as 'Can we measure a significant difference in self-reported anxiety and depression scores among students who use social media for more than X hours per day compared to those who employ it less?' Outline questions in a manner that allows for comparisons as 'What are the differences in mental health outcomes between students who mainly employ social media for academic purposes vs. those who employ it for social relations and entertainment?' Break the research into multiple questions if needed. This can help to explore diverse aspects of the topic as 'How does social media usage impact sleep patterns among students and how does this, consecutively, influence mental health outcomes?'

1.4 Formulation of Research Hypotheses

Identify the variables that you are interested in studying. These could be independent variables (manipulate or observe) and dependent variables (measured as outcomes).

Before formulating the hypothesis, review the existing literature to observe what is already recognized about the association between the variables. This will facilitate to build on existing knowledge and identify gaps.

Decide whether the researcher anticipates a positive or negative association between the variables. Will an increase in one variable cause an increase or decrease in the other?

A hypothesis should be precise and clear-cut. Avoid unclear statements that don't define the variables or the usual relationship.

Outline the hypothesis using lucid and brief language. Avoid jargon that might puzzle readers.

The hypothesis should be testable through empirical research. This means the researcher can design an experiment or gather data to either support or reject the hypothesis.

Make sure that the hypothesis is not unclear. It should state a clear association between variables that can be evaluated without bias.

A widespread format for stating a research hypothesis is the "if-then" structure. It joins the independent variable to the dependent variable and predicts the outcome.

Researchers can also formulate a null hypothesis (H0), which states that there is no significant relationship between the variables. Your research hypothesis (Ha) proposes the opposite.

Ensure that the research hypothesis is related to the research area and has the potential to contribute to existing knowledge.

Relate the hypothesis to relevant theoretical frameworks or models whenever applicable. This shows that the study is grounded in established concepts.

Example: Investigating the Effects of Social Media Usage on the Mental Health of Students

Research hypothesis: Before forming a hypothesis, it is essential to review existing literature to know what is already identified and make out gaps in knowledge. Then identify the independent variable: social media usage and the dependent variable: the mental health of students. Begin with a general statement about the association between social media usage and mental health as 'there is a significant relationship between social media usage and the mental health of students'. State whether anticipate a positive or negative association or if there is no significant association as 'increased social media usage is positively associated with declining mental health in students'. If other factors may persuade the association, a researcher might want to consider them as 'the association between social media usage and mental health in students is moderated by the level of social support they receive'. Make sure that the hypothesis is unambiguous and testable. It should be somewhat that researchers can calculate and analyze statistically as 'students who spend more than X hours per day on social media are more expected to account for higher levels of anxiety and depression compared to those who spend less time'. Thereafter, state the population to which the hypothesis applies like among undergraduate students in a college. Finally, the null hypothesis symbolizes the nonexistence of a consequence as 'there is no significant association between social media usage and the mental health of students'.

1.5 Formulation of Research Problem

Identify the wide-ranging research area or field in which are interested. This could be based on the research interests, previous studies, or emerging trends.

Review existing literature in the selected research area. Identify what has previously been studied, what questions have been addressed, and where there are gaps or unanswered issues.

Confine the focus within the research area. Think about exact aspects, variables, or dimensions that have not been meticulously explored or require further study.

Formulate questions that reflect the interest in the research area. These questions can help shape the research problem.

The research problem should emphasize a gap in knowledge, an inconsistency in findings, or an unanswered question that requires addressing.

The research problem should be lucid and precise, avoiding unclear language or broad statements. It should address a well-defined topic.

Make sure that the research problem is pertinent to the field and has significance in terms of contributing new knowledge, solving a problem, or advancing theory.

Consider how the research problem might have practical applications or real-world implications. This can improve the importance of the study.

Think about whether the research problem is realistic given the available resources, time, and expertise.

Describe why the research problem is important and what makes it valuable to investigate. Emphasize its potential impact on the field or society.

Observe the research problem from numerous angles. How do different stakeholders, disciplines, or theoretical frameworks view the issue?

Share the formulated research problem with supervisors, peers, or advisors. Their feedback can help to refine and progress it.

Example: Investigating the Effects of Social Media Usage on the Mental Health of Students

Research problem: There is a research gap in the existing literature about the distinctive effects of social media usage on the mental health of students.

While there is a considerable number of works on social media and mental health, little attention has been given to understanding how the duration, content, and peer interactions on social media platforms particularly impact the emotional well-being of students. This research aims to investigate the impact of social media usage on the mental health of students, focusing on the exact factors of time spent, content consumed, and peer interfaces. By analyzing these characteristics, we seek to give a comprehensive understanding of how social media influences the happiness of students.

1.6 Formulation of Research Objective

The research objectives should directly address the research problem that has been identified by the researcher. Each objective should contribute to resolving or exploring the problem.

Each objective should be unambiguous and focused on an exacting feature of the research. Avoid unclear or general statements.

Begin each objective with a clear action verb that designates what the researcher intends to achieve, namely, investigate, analyze, compare, identify, evaluate, etc.

Quantify the research objectives with exact measures, quantities, or criteria. This adds accuracy to the research plans.

Sort out the objectives hierarchically. Begin with broader objectives and then break them down into more specific sub-objectives.

Ensure that the objectives cover diverse aspects of the study. This could include methodology, collection of data, analysis, and possible outcomes.

The research objectives should directly connect the research questions that have been formulated. Each objective should answer, contribute to, or address a specific research question.

Make sure that the research objectives are realistic and reachable within the constraints of resources, time, and knowledge.

Organize the research objectives in a logical order that follows the development of the research study. This helps make a rational narrative for the study.

Be sensible about what the researcher can achieve within the scope of the study. Aggressive objectives might cause challenges during the research process.

Think about the possible impact of achieving each objective. How does it add to addressing the research problem or advancing the field?

Example: Investigating the Effects of Social Media Usage on the Mental Health of Students

Research objective: Start with a broad, overarching objective that abridges the main objective of the study as 'to investigate the effects of social media usage on the mental health of students'. Break the general objective into specific characteristics that want to investigate. Think about variables such as frequency, duration, and type of social media usage 'to examine the association between the frequency and duration of social media usage and the mental health outcomes of college students'. Undoubtedly state what intend to evaluate. Identify the mental health outcomes that are interested in, such as anxiety levels, depression symptoms, or overall well-being 'to assess the impact of social media usage on self-reported anxiety and depression scores among college students'. Define the population that are studying. This adds clearness and context to the objectives 'to understand how social media usage influences the mental well-being of college students'. If appropriate, include factors that may influence the association between social media usage and mental health as 'to explore the moderating role of social support from friends and family in the association between social media usage and mental health outcomes in college students'. Break down the research into numerous objectives if essential. This allows tackling diverse aspects of the topic 'to analyze the distinctions in mental health outcomes between students who mainly employ social media for academic principles and those who employ it for social interaction and entertainment'. Make sure that the objectives focus on the research questions that have been formulated. This makes sure that the study is purposeful and focused. Make sure that the objectives are realistic and achievable within the scope of the study.

1.7 Steps of Research Methodology

Select a research design that best fits the research goals. Select the design that aligns with the research questions and the nature of the research area.

Choose the methods the researcher will use to collect data. This could entail surveys, experiments, interviews, observations, content analysis, case studies, or a mixture of these.

Identify the target population and select a suitable sampling method. Whether researchers are using random sampling, stratified sampling, convenience sampling, or another method, explain how the researcher will certify the sample is representative.

Identify the tools the researcher will use to collect data, for instance, questionnaires, interview protocols, observation forms, or existing scales. Discuss how the researcher will validate and pre-test these instruments.

Specify the steps the researcher will take to collect data. Incorporate instructions for administering surveys, conducting interviews, or carrying out observations. Explain how the researcher will maintain consistency and standardization.

Define the variables the researcher is studying and how the researcher will measure them.

Describe the operational definitions and scales researchers will use.

Outline the methods researchers will use to analyze the collected data. For quantitative research, this could involve statistical techniques. For qualitative research, describe how researchers will code, categorize, and analyze the data.

Discuss any ethical issues related to the research and explain how researchers will address these concerns.

Describe how the researcher will ensure the validity (accuracy) and reliability (consistency) of the data collection methods.

Outline how the researcher will interpret the collected data. Discuss how researchers will link the findings back to the research questions or hypotheses.

Offer a timeline for each phase of the research, from data collection to data analysis and reporting. Make sure the timeline is sensible and attainable.

List the resources researchers will need for the research.

Elucidate how researchers will organize and manage the data during and after the research process. Discuss data storage, backup procedures, and data security.

Recognize any potential limitations of the methodology, for example, sample size constraints, selection bias, or the incapability to control all variables.

Mention whether researchers will conduct a pilot study to test and refine the research methods before the main study.

Give the rationale for each feature of the selected methodology. Explain why researchers have particular precise techniques, processes, and instruments.

Example: Investigating the Effects of Social Media Usage on the Mental Health of Students

Research methodology: Select a suitable research design based on the research question. Common designs for this type of study include cross-sectional, longitudinal, or experimental designs. Define the target population (undergraduate students) and determine the sample size. Think about using random or stratified sampling techniques to ensure representativeness. Undoubtedly define the independent variable (social media usage) and dependent variables (mental health outcomes). Recognize how it will determine them (self-report surveys, clinical interviews, physiological measures, etc.). Make out and validate the tools or instruments that will be employed to collect data. This might include validated surveys or scales for measuring social media usage and mental health. Delineate the methods for data collection. Incorporate details on recruitment, informed consent, and data collection sessions. Think about any moral considerations and methods for ensuring participant privacy. Carry out a pilot study to test the practicability and reliability of the instruments and procedures. Regulate the methodology based on the findings from the pilot. Identify the statistical or qualitative analysis techniques that will be employed. Explain how will interpret the data to tackle the research questions. Undoubtedly state the criteria for concluding and the implications of the findings. Argue the steps that are taken to certify the validity and reliability of the study. Recognize and thrash out potential limitations of the study. This could include limitations in the sample size, the generalizability of findings, or any biases in the data collection methods.

1.8 Steps of Data Collection

Review the research objectives and questions to comprehend what kind of data the researcher needs to collect. Establish the types of variables, measurements, and information that will address the research goals.

Choose the most appropriate data collection methods based on the research design.

Build up well-structured and clear survey questions that confine pertinent information. Utilize a mix of question types (closed-ended and open-ended) to collect quantitative and qualitative data.

Arrange interview procedures with open-ended questions that support participants to sophisticate on their experiences, viewpoints, or insights.

Make observation procedures that outline what researchers will observe, how researchers will record it, and any precise criteria researchers are seeking.

Delineate the experimental methods including the manipulation of variables, the control group, and the experimental group.

Identify the categories or subjects researchers will be looking for in the content analysis and how researchers will code and analyze the data.

Identify the variables researchers are studying and how researchers will measure them. Afford functioning definitions for concepts that might have diverse understandings.

Choose the sampling technique and find out the sample size. Explain how researchers will access and approach prospective participants.

Before implementing the data collection plan, carry out a pilot test. This entails trying out the data collection mechanisms on a small group to make out any issues or ambiguities.

Summarize the step-by-step methods for collecting data. This comprises instructions for administering surveys, conducting interviews, making observations, or conducting experiments.

Specify measures researchers will take to ensure data quality, for example, interrater reliability tests, training of data collectors, and checking for consistency.

Thrash out ethical considerations associated with data collection.

Describe how researchers will organize, store, and manage the collected data. Explain the data coding process, if relevant, and talk about any software researchers will employ to manage data.

Summarize any checks or validations researchers will carry out to certify the accuracy and integrity of the collected data.

Present a schedule for data collection activities indicating when and how data will be collected. Ensure the timeline aligns with the research objectives and generally project timeline.

List the resources researchers will need for data collection and estimate the costs associated with data collection.

Anticipate possible challenges that might happen during data collection and summarize contingency plans to address them.

Keep comprehensive documentation of the data collection methods, instruments, and any changes made during the procedure. This documentation will be important for clearness and replicability.

Example: Investigating the Effects of Social Media Usage on the Mental Health of Students

Data collection: Describe the independent variable (social media usage) and dependent variables (mental health outcomes) and state the aspects of social media usage that are interested in and the mental health measures that plan to use. Select suitable measurement tools or instruments for collecting data. This might include validated surveys or scales for assessing social media usage and mental health and making sure that the instruments have been used and validated in related studies. Carry out a pre-test of the instruments to identify any issues with clearness or respondent comprehension and pursue this with a pilot study involving a small sample to assess the feasibility and reliability of the instruments. Clearly describe the target population (undergraduate students) and find out the sample size. Consider using random or stratified sampling methods to certify representativeness. Build up a recruitment strategy. This could entail distributing invitations through college channels, using social media platforms, or collaborating with pertinent student groups. Converse the purpose of the study and the benefits of participation. Develop an informed consent form outlining the purpose of the study, procedures, risks, benefits, and the right to withdraw and ensure participants have a clear understanding and give written consent. Delineate step-by-step practices for data collection and comprise details on how participants will access and complete surveys, the duration of data collection, and any specific instructions they need to follow. Include questions to collect socio-demographic information about participants, such as age, gender, academic major, and year of study. This information can be useful for subgroup analyses. If the study involves self-reported social media usage, ask participants about the platforms they use, the frequency and duration of usage, and the purpose (academic, social, and entertainment). Manage the preferred mental health assessments. This could involve standardized surveys or scales assessing anxiety, depression, stress, or overall well-being. Make sure that participants receive obvious and brief instructions for completing the surveys or assessments and comprise any specific details about the time frame for reporting social media usage or recalling mental health experiences. Execute a system for sending reminders to participants to complete the surveys and follow-up emails or messages to improve response rates as well as apply measures to ensure data quality. This could involve checking for completeness, consistency, and validity of responses. Sketch how will protect participant data and specify who will have access to the data and how it will be stored securely. Predict possible challenges or unexpected circumstances and develop contingency plans. This might include technical issues, low response rates, or unanticipated participant reactions.

1.9 Steps of Variable Selection

Gain a bottomless understanding of the research area or topic. This includes reviewing existing literature, understanding pertinent theories, and identifying main ideas.

Elucidate the research objectives. What exact information do researchers need to collect to answer the research questions or test your hypotheses?

Find out which variables are independent (predictors) and which are dependent (outcomes). Independent variables are factors the researcher can manipulate or observe, whereas dependent variables are the ones the researcher measures.

Select variables that are directly pertinent to the research area and objectives. Avoid such variables that don't have a clear relationship to the study.

Make sure that the variables are well-defined and theoretically clear. Vagueness in variable definitions can bring about confusion and wrong data collection.

Give operational definitions for each variable. These definitions denote how each variable will be measured or observed substantially.

If the research is grounded in a theoretical framework, select variables that focus on the concepts and constructs of that framework.

Think about the viability of measuring or observing the selected variables. Make sure that the required data can be collected within the available resources, time, and knowledge.

Select variables that have established validity and reliability.

Avoid multiple variables that determine the identical concept. Redundant variables can confuse data analysis and explanation.

For each variable, describe why it is significant for the study. Validate its inclusion based on its significance to the research questions and the existing knowledge in the field.

Be aware of possible confounding variables—those that might persuade the association between the independent and dependent variables. Decide whether to control for these confounders or include them in the research study.

The pilot test is required on selected variables to make sure that they are sensible to evaluate and that participants understand them as intended.

Depending on the research design, think about whether the variables should be measured at a single point in time or need to collect data longitudinally.

Keep the study's scope in mind. Too many variables might make the study multifaceted and hard to analyze efficiently.

Make sure that the selected variables adjust to ethical considerations. Avoid variables that might violate participants' rights.

Example: Investigating the Effects of Social Media Usage on the Mental Health of Students

Variable selection: Unmistakably articulate the research question or questions. This will direct the identification of important variables and distinguish between the independent variable (social media usage) and the dependent variable (mental health outcomes). Carry out a literature review to recognize established measures and definitions for social media usage and mental health as well as consider how earlier studies have approached these variables. Then define and operationalize each variable as if social media usage is the independent variable, and state how it will compute it (hours per day, types of platforms, purpose of usage). Select validated measurement tools or instruments for assessing social media usage and mental health and make sure that these tools have been used in earlier research and are suitable for the study population. Identify that social media usage and mental health are composite constructs with multiple dimensions. For social media usage, consider factors such as frequency, duration, types of content, and the purpose of usage. For mental health, consider anxiety, depression, stress, and overall well-being. Integrate socio-demographic variables into the study. These could include age, gender, academic major, year of study, and other pertinent characteristics that may influence social media usage and mental health. If the study considers moderating or mediating variables, clearly identify and include them in the variable selection. For example, if social support moderates the association between social media usage and mental health, include a measure of social support. If the study involves a longitudinal design, cautiously consider the temporal aspect of the variables. For example, assess changes in social media usage and mental health over time. Identify that social media usage and mental health can be influenced by cultural and contextual factors and ensure that the variables capture these nuances, particularly if the study entails a different population. Before finalizing the variables, carry out pilot testing to make sure that the measurement tools are clear, reliable, and valid and regulate the variables based on the findings from the pilot study. Unambiguously document the selected variables, their definitions, and how they will be measured in the research practice. This documentation certifies consistency throughout the study.

1.10 Selection of Data Types

Describe the research objectives and questions. What exact information does the researcher need to collect to address these objectives?

If the research plans to measure associations, patterns, or trends, quantitative data might be suitable. This type of data involves numerical values that can be measured and analyzed statistically.

Quantitative data can be obtained through structured surveys with closed-ended questions. Controlled experiments often make quantitative data, allowing for statistical analysis. Researchers can quantify observational data by counting occurrences or measuring attributes.

If researchers aspire to survey meanings, perceptions, experiences, or contexts, qualitative data might be more appropriate. This type of data involves non-numerical information that is often text-based.

Qualitative data can be collected through in-depth interviews that allow participants to share their perceptions.

Group discussions give qualitative insights into shared perspectives and interactions.

Qualitative observations entail capturing nuances and contextual details that might not be quantifiable.

In several cases, using both quantitative and qualitative data can give a more widespread understanding of the research area. This approach is acknowledged as mixed-methods research.

Think about whether existing datasets, databases, or records can give the data the researcher needs. Secondary data sources can be precious for certain research topics.

Consider data triangulation, which involves collecting multiple types of data to validate findings and improve the depth of analysis.

Think about the available resources. Quantitative research needs data collection tools, software, and statistical knowledge. Qualitative research may require interview or observation talents.

The research design will influence the type of collected data.

Think about what participants is comfortable sharing. Some persons might be more inclined to give numerical reactions, whereas others might choose to express their experiences in qualitative terms.

Make a decision whether researchers need widespread, quantitative data that covers a wide range of participants or qualitative data that investigates intensely the experiences of a smaller group.

Ensure that the selection of data type aligns with ethical considerations and respects participants' rights.

Diverse research areas might lend themselves better to definite types of data.

Example: Investigating the Effects of Social Media Usage on the Mental Health of Students

Data types: Distinguish between qualitative and quantitative data. Qualitative data may comprise textual information, whilst quantitative data involves numerical measurements. Clearly describe each variable and state its type. For example, the independent variable: is social media usage, and its type: is quantitative (hours per day, frequency of use), and the dependent variable: is mental health outcomes, and its type: is quantitative (scores on anxiety and depression scales). If working with quantitative data, recognize the measurement scales for each variable. For example, social media usage: ratio scale (measuring hours per day) and anxiety and depression scores: interval or ratio scales (depending on the measurement instrument). Identify any categorical variables that may be part of the study, such as gender, academic major, or types of social media platforms used. If the study involves a temporal aspect, describe time-related data and state the format for recording time, such as dates or specific time intervals. If incorporating qualitative data (open-ended survey responses, interview transcripts), delineate the type of information that aims to collect and specify the thematic analysis, content analysis, or other qualitative data analysis methods. If using a mixed methods approach, clearly articulate how quantitative and qualitative data will be integrated and explain the associations between the two types of data and how they will inform each other. For socio-demographic variables, describe the types of data that will be collected (gender, age) and their particular formats (categorical, numerical). If appropriate, explain the coding system that will be employed for numerical or categorical values. This is principally significant when working with qualitative data. Conduct pilot testing to make sure that the data types are suitable and the data collection instruments confine the intended information precisely as well as delineate procedures for ensuring data quality including ensures for completeness, accuracy, and consistency. State how missing data will be handled. Document the data types, measurement scales, and any related details in the research protocol. This documentation gives a reference for consistency throughout the study. Constantly observe the data collection procedure and be open to adapting the approach if unanticipated challenges or opportunities take place.

1.11 Selection of Appropriate Statistical Tools

Define the research objectives and questions. What unambiguous insights are seeking to gain from the data analysis?

Think whether the data is quantitative, qualitative, or mixed-methods. Different statistical techniques are suited for diverse data types.

The research design will direct the selection of statistical techniques, such as, experiments often engage hypothesis testing, whereas longitudinal studies might entail growth curve modeling.

If the researcher has specific hypotheses, identify whether they are about relationships, differences, trends, or predictions. The nature of the hypotheses will inform the choice of statistical tests.

The size of the sample can influence the statistical tools the researcher can use. Several methods need larger sample sizes for reliable results.

Consider the distribution of the data. If the data follows a normal distribution, certain parametric tests might be proper. Non-parametric tests can be employed for non-normally distributed data.

Think about the nature of variables that are nominal, ordinal, interval, or ratio level. Different statistical methods are appropriate for different levels of measurement.

Identify whether researchers are looking to describe the data, compare groups, predict outcomes, explore associations, or determine patterns. Different objectives need diverse statistical approaches.

Select statistical tools that researchers are well-known with or eager to learn.

If researchers have multiple dependent and independent variables, researcher might require employing multivariate analysis methods.

If the data entails temporal trends, time series analysis methods will be relevant. ANOVA and regression techniques are generally used for examining associations between variables and testing hypotheses. Chi-square and Fisher's exact tests are used for analyzing categorical data. Correlation and Covariance analysis are appropriate for examining relationships between variables and assessing the strength and direction of associations. Content analysis, thematic analysis, and coding schemes are useful for qualitative data. Factor Analysis and Principal Component Analysis are used for reducing multifaceted data sets into more convenient components and identifying fundamental patterns.

Select methods that adapt to ethical reflections and precisely symbolize the data without causing damage or misconception.

If researchers are unsure about which statistical techniques to use, consult with experienced researchers, Supervisors, or statisticians who know the particular research area.

Example: Investigating the Effects of Social Media Usage on the Mental Health of Students

Appropriate statistical tools: Noticeably articulate the research questions and hypotheses. This will guide the selection of statistical tools that can tackle the specific objectives. Consider the types of data that have been collected (quantitative, qualitative, or mixed methods) and their measurement scales. Statistical tools should be selected based on the nature of the data. Identify the independent variable (social media usage) and dependent variables (mental health outcomes). This difference is important for selecting appropriate statistical tests. Then recognize the design of the study (cross-sectional, longitudinal, and experimental). Different study designs may need different statistical approaches. Measure the normality of the quantitative (except ordinal and nominal) data. If the data is normally distributed, parametric tests may be appropriate. If not, consider non-parametric alternatives. For describing the data, choose proper descriptive statistics. This may include means, medians, standard deviations, or percentages, depending on the characteristics of the variables. Select inferential statistical tests based on the research questions and data types. Common tests for investigating the relationship between social media usage and mental health include correlation analysis for exploring associations between two continuous variables (Pearson or Spearman correlation), regression analysis for examining the predictive association between social media usage and mental health outcomes, t-tests or ANOVA for comparing means between groups if your study involves categorical variables, chi-square test for examining associations between categorical variables and multivariate analysis for multiple dependent variables or predictors. If the study involves examining moderation or mediation effects, consider moderation analysis or mediation analysis. Carry out a power analysis to find out the suitable sample size for the study. This ensures that the study has sufficient statistical power to detect meaningful effects if the assumptions of the selected statistical tests are met. For instance, check for homogeneity of variances, normality of residuals, and linearity assumptions. Consider the interpretability of results and select statistical tools that align with the ability to describe findings in a significant manner to the readers. For this, select statistical software that supports the tools that plan to use. Develop a strategy for handling missing data. This could involve imputation techniques or sensitivity analyses to assess the impact of missing data on results. If possible, talk to the statistician or data analyst to ensure that the selected statistical tools are suitable and applied accurately. Undoubtedly document the statistical methods used in the research protocol. This documentation is necessary for clearness and replication.

1.12 Analyzing the Data

Review the research questions, hypotheses, and the exact objectives of the study. Ensure there is an obvious on what I am aiming to study.

Clean the dataset by checking for errors, missing values, and outliers and address any issues that could impact the precision of the study. Then organize the dataset in a format that is appropriate for analysis, this may be using spreadsheets, statistical software, or particular tools. Bear in mind; to use the proper statistical techniques and their significance to the research objectives. Describe in brief how each technique was useful to the data.

Spell out the exact aims of the data analysis. If researchers are looking to illustrate patterns, test hypotheses, explore associations, or make predictions, select suitable statistical methods (descriptive statistics, inferential statistics, regression, correlation, t-tests, ANOVA, chi-square tests, etc.) based on research design, research questions, data types, and objectives.

Employ descriptive statistics to summarize and illustrate the data. If there is a sample and want to conclude a larger population, use inferential statistics, which includes hypothesis testing, confidence intervals, and p-values.

Generate graphs, charts, and visualizations to characterize the data, which includes histograms, scatter plots, bar charts, and line graphs can help to understand patterns and associations. Use the statistical software depending on the knowledge and the complication of the study. Carry out the particular statistical techniques on the data and deduce the results based on the objectives of the research. Pay attention to effect sizes and statistical significance. Thrash out the size and extent of the results that have been observed. If appropriate, compare effect sizes to highlight the significance of the findings.

Interpret the output from the analysis in the context of the research questions. Write what the findings suggest about the research topic. Include pertinent visuals to demonstrate the findings. Graphs and charts can make the results more logical and visually interesting. Present the findings in an apparent and organized manner using tables, charts, and graphs to visually characterize the results. Summarize the findings in a holistic approach. Explain how they jointly contribute to the broader perceptive of the research topic. Move towards the explanation with important thoughts and impartiality. Keep away from over-interpreting results or making arguments that go beyond what the data can support. Present the interpretation in an apparent, concise, and organized way. Use simple language to make sure that the findings are reachable to a broad audience.

If there are formulated hypotheses, compare the findings with these hypotheses to establish if they are supported or rejected. Attach each finding to the research questions or hypotheses that have been formulated. Explain whether the findings support or contradict them.

Over and above statistical significance, think about whether the results have practical importance or significance in the research area. Distinguish between statistical significance and practical significance. Statistical significance indicates whether an observed effect is likely to have occurred unintentionally, whereas practical significance spotlights the real-world significance of the effect.

Admit any limitations of the study, for example, sample size constraints, confounding variables, or potential biases. Address the limitations of the study that might have influenced the results. Discuss the potential implications of the findings for theory, practice, or policy. Analyze patterns, trends, or associations observed in the data. Are there any noteworthy trends that focus on the expectations?

If there are predictive models, think about cross-validation to measure the performance and generalizability of the model.

Discuss the reliability (consistency) and validity (accuracy) of the findings based on the methods that have been used.

Inscribe a narrative analysis of the findings, explaining what they mean in the situation of the research topic. Discuss how the findings contribute to existing knowledge in the research area. Reflect on any unexpected results and their implications. If the researcher encountered results that were unexpected or contradicted existing theories, thrash out potential reasons for these discrepancies. This demonstrates important thinking and a nuanced understanding of the research topic.

If the study is grounded in a theoretical framework, thrash out how the findings relate to or extend that framework.

If researchers are uncertain about data analysis, consult with experts, mentors, or statisticians who can give guidance and validation of the study. Compare the results to earlier studies in the same field. Discuss similarities, differences, and potential reasons for different findings.

Based on the findings, propose areas for further research. What questions remain unanswered or need deeper investigation?

Example: Investigating the Effects of Social Media Usage on the Mental Health of Students

Data analysis: Start by organizing the data and addressing any issues correlated to data entry errors, missing values, and outliers. Cleaning the data ensures that successive analyses are based on precise information. Determine descriptive statistics to sum up and explain the main features of the data. This may include means, medians, standard deviations, and percentages. Conduct exploratory data analysis to visually and statistically explore associations between social media usage and mental health outcomes. This might involve scatter plots, histograms, or other visualizations and employ correlation analysis to quantify the strength and direction of relationships between continuous variables (social media usage and mental health scores). If suitable, conduct regression analysis to examine the predictive association between social media usage (independent variable) and mental health outcomes (dependent variable), controlling for related covariates. If the study involves group comparisons (different levels of social media usage or different populations), use t-tests, ANOVA, or non-parametric equivalents to identify significant differences. If the study involves categorical variables (types of social media platforms used), use the chi-square test to examine associations between these variables. If hypothesize that certain factors moderate the association between social media usage and mental health, conduct moderation analysis to test these effects. If suspect that certain variables mediate the association between social media usage and mental health, conduct a mediation analysis to explore these pathways. If the study involves multiple dependent variables or predictors, consider multivariate analysis techniques such as MANOVA or multiple regression and use statistical software to carry out analyses efficiently and accurately. Select software based on familiarity and the specific requirements of the analyses. If there are covariates that might confound the association between social media usage and mental health, include them in the analyses to control for their upshots. Interpret the results of the analyses in the background of the research questions and hypotheses. Discuss the practical significance of findings, not just statistical significance. Make sure that the analyses meet the assumptions of the statistical tests that are used. If assumptions are violated, consider alternative analyses or transformations. Carry out sensitivity analyses to explore the impact of potential outliers or influential cases on the results. If the study involves mixed methods, integrate quantitative data with qualitative findings to give a comprehensive understanding of the research questions. Share the data analysis plan and results with mentors or statisticians for validation and advice. Document the whole data analysis procedure, including the exact statistical tests, parameters, and software used. This documentation ensures clearness and replicability. Describe conclusions based on the analyses and thrash out their implications for theory, practice, or future research. Present the findings in an obvious and planned way in the research report or thesis including tables, graphs, and visualizations to improve the lucidity of the results.

1.13 Drawing a Logical Conclusion

Summarize the most important findings of the study. Highlight the main results that directly address the research objectives.

Connect the findings to the research objectives that primarily aim to reach. Describe how every finding contributes to addressing those aims.

Thrash out how the findings align with or diverge from the research questions or hypotheses. Elucidate whether the study supports or contradicts the primary expectations.

If the study involved several analyses or diverse aspects, synthesize the results to give a consistent overview of what has been learned.

Reveal the implications of the findings for theory, practice, policy, or the broader pasture of research. How do the results move forward our perception of the topic?

Thrash out the practical significance of the findings beyond statistical implication. How do the results impact real-world conditions or decision-making?

If the study contributes to existing theoretical frameworks, models, or ideas, explain how it expands or confronts them.

Admit any limitations of the study that might have influenced the results. Be transparent about possible sources of prejudice or ambiguity.

Based on the findings and their limitations, suggest areas for future research. Consider what questions remain unreciprocated or need further exploration.

If the study introduced innovative manners, approaches, or viewpoints, highlight how these contribute to the field's development.

Revisit the primary research objects and thrash out how the study has fulfilled or extended them.

Summarize the conclusion by giving closure to the research journey. Highlight the implication of the study's contribution.

In conclusion, avoid over-generalizing beyond what the data supports. Attach to the scope and limitations of the study.

Remain the conclusion succinct and focused on the main takeaways from the research.

Conclude the research by leaving a permanent idea. End with a statement that underscores the value of the study and its significance to the field.

Talk about any personal growth, knowledge, or insights gained through the research process.

Make sure that it is well-written and free from errors. It should be a sophisticated and professional representation of the study's outcomes.

Example: Investigating the Effects of Social Media Usage on the Mental Health of Students

Logical conclusion: Start by summarizing the major findings of the study and present a concise overview of the results linked to social media usage and its impact on the mental health of students. Refer back to the research questions and hypotheses and assess how well the study addressed these questions and whether the findings support or contradict the initial hypotheses. Identify and thrash out any patterns or trends observed in the data and emphasize significant associations or differences between groups and their implications for understanding the effects of social media usage on mental health. Distinguish between statistical significance and practical significance and if a result is statistically significant does not essentially mean it has practical importance. Discuss the practical implications of the findings. If relevant, deduce effect sizes to give a more nuanced understanding of the magnitude of observed effects. This helps in assessing the practical significance of the results. Explain any limitations of the study. This might include issues correlated to sample size, generalizability, measurement tools, or other constraints that could impact the validity and applicability of the findings. Compare the findings with existing literature and argue how the results align with or diverge from previous research on the association between social media usage and mental health in student populations. Deal with alternative explanations for the findings and describe whether other factors or variables could have influenced the observed associations and how these factors might be considered in future studies. Discuss the practical implications of the study for diverse stakeholders including students, educators, policymakers, and mental health professionals, and think how the findings could inform interventions or policies. Offer recommendations for future research based on the gaps and limitations identified in the study. Recommend paths for further investigation that could enhance our understanding of the topic. Emphasize the contributions of the study to the broader field of research. Highlight how the findings add new insights, challenge existing ideas, or suggest practical applications. Narrate the conclusions back to the objectives of the study. Measure how well the goals are and whether the study gives precious contributions to the research area. If suitable, propose practical recommendations based on the findings. This could include suggestions for educational programs, mental health support services, or social media usage directives for students. Craft clear and concise conclusions keep away from introducing new information in the conclusion and focus on summarizing and interpreting the results. Integrate the well-formulated conclusions into the final research report, ensuring a consistent and logical flow from the introduction to the conclusion.

1.14 Writing the Policy Implications

Summarize the main findings of the study. Emphasize the main results that have the most significant policy implications.

Connect the findings to the research objectives that aimed to accomplish. Describe how each finding unswervingly addresses those objectives.

Find out who the key stakeholders are that would be interested in the research findings. This could include government agencies, organizations, support groups, or society members.

Highlight the practical significance of the findings beyond statistical significance. Thrash out how the results can cause significant changes in policies or practices.

Based on the findings, give understandable and actionable recommendations for policy changes or improvements. These recommendations should be exact, realistic, and aligned with the research outcomes.

Describe the background in which the recommendations are relevant. Explain the current policy background, existing practices, and any pertinent challenges or opportunities.

Delineate the possible benefits and positive outcomes that could result from implementing the policy recommendations. Employ evidence from the study to support these claims.

Predict prospective concerns or objections to the recommendations. Address any challenges, problems, or counterarguments and propose strategies to moderate them.

Measure the viability of implementing the recommendations. Think about factors for example resources, political considerations, and sensibleness.

Present a step-by-step guide for how the recommendations can be executed. Outline precise actions, timelines, and answerable parties.

Enumerate the possible impact of the recommendations in terms of costs saved, lives improved, or other measurable outcomes.

Back up the recommendations with references to the study's findings and other pertinent research. This improves the integrity of the suggestions.

Think about involving pertinent stakeholders in the progress of the policy recommendations. Combined efforts can improve the possibility of flourishing implementation.

Employ clear, succinct, and jargon-free language to communicate the policy implications. Create the recommendations reachable to a wider audience.

If there are multiple recommendations, prioritize them based on their possible impact and practicability. Emphasize the most significant changes first.

Make sure that the recommendations are based exclusively on the research findings and knowledge. Keep away from making claims that extend beyond the study's scope.

Example: Investigating the Effects of Social Media Usage on the Mental Health of Students

Policy implications: Identify the policymakers or stakeholders who are the primary readers for the policy implications and shape the recommendations to the level and scope of the policy viewers, whether it is at the institutional, educational, or governmental level. Begin by summarizing the major findings of the study that are related to policy considerations. Communicate the main results connected to social media usage and its impact on the mental health of students. Bond the research findings to broader policy goals or objectives. Reveal how addressing the issues identified in the study focuses on larger aims such as improving student well-being, enhancing educational outcomes, or fostering a healthier online environment. Identify decisive areas for policy intervention based on the findings. Identify specific aspects of social media usage or mental health outcomes that are particularly salient and require attention. Devise exact and targeted policy recommendations and shape the suggestions to address the nuances of the research findings. If too much social media use is associated with negative mental health outcomes, advocate policies promoting digital literacy education and time-management strategies. If specific social media platforms are linked to exacting mental health issues, think about suggesting platform-specific guidelines. Predict and argue potential barriers to implementing proposed policies. This might include resource constraints, legal considerations, or resistance from various stakeholders. Offer strategies for overcoming these barriers. If feasible, include input from related stakeholders in the policy-making process. Consult with educators, mental health professionals, students, and other key groups to ensure a widespread and practical approach. Focus on precautionary measures and support systems and emphasize policies that encourage proactive approaches to nurturing positive mental health and mitigating potential harms associated with social media use. Put forward the performance of educational programs for students, parents, and educators. These could focus on promoting responsible social media use, digital well-being, and strategies for maintaining positive mental health.

1.15 Writing the Societal Implications

Summarize the most important findings of the study. Emphasize the results that have the main potential to influence society.

Connect the findings to the research goals that they set out to accomplish. Describe how each finding unswervingly addresses those objectives.

Analyze how the study's findings relate to broader societal concerns, challenges, trends, or desires. Think about how they adapt to public interests and apprehensions.

Highlight the practical significance of the findings beyond statistical significance. Thrash out how the results can contribute optimistically to society.

Delineate the prospective benefits and positive outcomes that could result from the application of the study's findings in society. Employ evidence from the research to support these claims.

Consider how the findings can address or improve societal challenges, for example, environmental issues, inequality, or economic apprehensions.

If the findings put forward opportunities for positive change, advocate for those changes by describing how they adjust to societal values and happiness.

Employ the research to lift awareness about issues that might not have received much attention. Argue how the findings shed light on lesser-known apprehensions.

Deal with any ethical considerations related to the findings and their possible societal applications. Thrash out how ethical standards should direct their implementation.

Think about engaging with stakeholders from diverse sectors of society to collect input on the possible implications of the research.

Be transparent about the limitations of the study and how they might influence the application of the findings in society.

If the research involves cultural or social backgrounds, think about how the findings can value and support cultural understanding.

Inscribe in a method that makes the findings and implications reachable to broad viewers, including those who may not have a condition in the field.

Think about how the research findings can encourage inclusivity, diversity, and equal access to promote within society.

Emphasize areas where further research is required to fully comprehend the societal implications of the findings. Promote others to persist in exploring the topic.

Example: Investigating the Effects of Social Media Usage on the Mental Health of Students

Societal implications: start by giving a summary of the study's major findings. Outline the results in a manner that is reachable to wider viewers beyond academia. Clearly articulate why the study is related to society at large and explain how social media and mental health are significant topics that influence individuals, communities, and societal well-being. Highlight the need for public awareness and education regarding the possible impact of social media on mental health. Write the findings in a manner that contributes to a better-informed society. Suggest increased digital literacy programs in schools, workplaces, and community settings and cheer society to develop skills for responsible and mindful social media use. Encourage the idea of making informed decisions about social media use and encourage individuals to be aware of the possible effects on their mental health and to accept strategies for responsible consumption. Emphasize the role of communities, both online and offline, in supporting individuals' mental health support the formation of positive and supportive online spaces, and emphasize the significance of offline communities. If the study identifies issues connected to cyberbullying or online harassment, suggest policies and societal initiatives that tackle and check these behaviors. Highlight the significance of creating a safe online environment and supporting inclusivity in digital spaces. Emphasize the prospective negative impact of exclusion or discrimination on mental health and advocate for inclusive practices online. Put forward for increased accessibility to mental health support services and stress the significance of having resources available for individuals who may be struggling with mental health issues exacerbated by social media exercise.

1.16 Write the Scope for Future Research

Succinct the key findings of the current study. This gives a background for the areas that require further study.

Thrash out the gaps, limitations, and unanswered questions that emerged from the research. What characteristics were not fully covered because of limitations or unexpected findings?

Narrate the gaps and limitations to the research goals that primarily set out to be accomplished. How do these gaps relate to the broader research area?

Based on the gaps and limitations, recommend exact research directions that could be pursued in the future. Emphasize the possible significance of these areas.

Think about whether future research should widen the scope to include associated areas or narrow it down to focus on particular subtopics.

Create particular research questions that could be addressed in prospect studies. These questions should take place logically from the gaps identified in the current research.

If the study exposed methodological challenges, propose how future research could overcome these challenges or suggest alternative techniques.

Point out any promising trends, technologies, or expansions in the field that could disclose new avenues for research.

Propose how future research could expand or challenge existing theories, models, or frameworks based on the findings of the study.

Recognize particular aspects of the research topic that were not fully addressed in the study.

Thrash out why these aspects are significant for an inclusive understanding.

Explore the possibility of interdisciplinary or cross-disciplinary research that could give new insights into the topic.

If the study produces new hypotheses or unanticipated findings, thrash out how these could direct future analyses.

If there are multiple suggestions, prioritize them based on their possible impact and viability. Emphasize the great areas for further study.

Think about how future research suggests practical implications, contributes to policy, or tackles real-world challenges.

Recommend areas where association among researchers from diverse disciplines or institutions could improve the depth and breadth of future study.

Give confidence to future researchers to explore novel approaches, methodologies, or technologies that can drive the boundaries of understanding in the field.

Example: Investigating the Effects of Social Media Usage on the Mental Health of Students

Scope for future research: Start by acknowledging the limitations of the study and explain any constraints, challenges, or aspects that were not fully addressed in the study. Make out unanswered questions or areas where the study may have raised new inquiries. Think about aspects of social media usage and mental health that were not fully explored or unexpected findings that warrant further investigation. Conduct a meticulous review of existing literature to identify gaps or emerging trends in the field and measure how the study adds to the existing body of knowledge and where there is room for further study. Specify new research questions that emerge from your study. These questions should build upon the findings and limitations of your current research, addressing gaps in understanding or providing deeper insights. Put forward alternative study designs that could improve understanding. For example, if the study was cross-sectional, consider proposing a longitudinal study to explore changes in social media usage and mental health over time. Consider exploring the effects of social media on the mental health of students within specific demographic groups. This could include investigating differences based on age, gender, socioeconomic status, or cultural background. Suggest studies that investigate moderating factors that may influence the association between social media usage and mental health. This could include factors such as social support, coping mechanisms, or individual resilience. Recommend research that explores the efficiency of intervention strategies aimed at mitigating negative effects and promoting positive outcomes. This might involve educational programs, digital well-being initiatives, or counseling services. Support future research to consider cultural variations in the effects of social media on mental health and examine how cultural norms and values persuade the impact of online interactions.

1.17 Importance of External Validity

External validity certifies that research findings have significance and practical applicability beyond the pressing study background. This is essential for making informed decisions and policies in real-world conditions.

The crucial objective of research is often to create significant statements about a larger population or broader situation. Strong external validity facilitates researchers to generalize their findings to populations or conditions beyond the study sample.

Research with high external validity can impact a wider range of stakeholders including policymakers, practitioners, and the general readers. Findings that relate to a broader perspective are expected to have a long-lasting influence.

External validity supports the validity of research claims by demonstrating that the findings are not restricted to an exact group or condition, but have significance for different settings.

Externally valid research contributes to a deeper perception of fundamental principles, associations, and phenomena that expand beyond the narrow confines of the study.

Conducting research in diverse backgrounds or with diverse populations helps cross-validate findings. If results consistently hold accurate across various situations, their robustness and trustworthiness increase.

External validity is important for informing policy decisions. Policymakers need to know if findings from an unambiguous study can be trustworthy to show actions on a larger scale.

If research findings are externally valid, resources can be allocated more efficiently based on the perceptive that related outcomes can be accepted in diverse circumstances.

External validity is strictly related to the replicability of research. If findings are externally valid, other researchers should be capable of replicating the study's outcomes in diverse conditions.

Research findings that are externally valid help ensure that decisions are reasonable and unbiased for a broader scope of individuals or groups.

External validity supports researchers in designing studies that tackle questions with significance beyond a narrow scope, contributing to the expansion of science and knowledge.

Research with strong external validity can encourage new avenues of study and innovation. Researchers can build on established findings to investigate new areas.

Example: Investigating the Effects of Social Media Usage on the Mental Health of Students

External validity: Unmistakably describe the characteristics of the student population under study and incorporate details of age, educational level, geographic location, and any other related demographic information. Measure the diversity within the sample and ensure that the study includes participants from different backgrounds, cultures, and social contexts to improve the generalizability of the findings. Give a rationale for why the particular sample is representative of the larger population of interest. Thrash out any potential biases or limitations in the sampling approach. If appropriate to the research question, certify that the sample includes several social media users. Diverse platforms and usage patterns may have exclusive effects on mental health. Consider the socioeconomic status of the participants. Identify that the effects of social media on mental health may differ among students from diverse economic backgrounds. Measure the types of educational settings represented in the study. Think about whether the findings are exact to definite types of institutions (universities vs. colleges). Consider the cultural background of the study and identify that the effects of social media on mental health may be influenced by cultural norms, values, and attitudes toward technology. If the study involves participants at diverse developmental stages, consider how age may influence the relationship between social media usage and mental health upshots. If feasible, include longitudinal studies to measure the stability of the observed effects over time. This improves the external validity of the findings by demonstrating the robustness of associations. Without a doubt identify the contextual factors pertinent to the study. This may include the exact characteristics of social media use, the incidence of definite mental health issues, and the availability of support services in the specified background. Identify possible temporal factors that may influence the generalizability of the findings. Social media platforms, usage patterns, and societal attitudes toward mental health can change over time. Consider the transferability of the findings to diverse settings. Measure whether the observed effects of social media on mental health are expected to be similar in other educational or cultural situations. Clearly describe the exclusion and inclusion criteria for participants. This helps in identifying the boundaries of the study and clarifies to which populations the findings can be generalized. Recognize prospective limitations that may impact external validity. This could include issues related to sample size, participant selection, or the unique characteristics of the study population. Document the methodological details of the study including data collection methods, measurement instruments, and any technical information that may impact the generalizability of the results. Support researchers to replicate the study in diverse backgrounds or with diverse populations. Replication studies add to the external validity by assessing the consistency of findings across different settings. Compare the study population and background with other appropriate studies. Thrash out the similarities and distinctions, highlighting factors that may influence the generalizability of the findings. Differentiate between transferability and generalizability where transferability means the applicability of findings to related backgrounds and generalizability implies broader applicability to diverse populations. Be conscious of changes in the social media background and recognize that new platforms may come out and existing platforms may go forward, potentially influencing the applicability of the findings to future circumstances. If suitable, employ different analytical methods that improve the robustness of the results. For example, using both quantitative and qualitative techniques can give a more widespread understanding of the occurrence. This can augment the external validity of the study on the effects of social media usage on the mental health of students and give a solid base for future researchers to build upon.

2. Writing the Introduction and Literature Review

2.1 Introduction

The introduction and literature review are the introductory parts of any academic or research study. Set the phase for the study, providing the situation, background, and a clear understanding of the research problem are provided. In this section, break down the whole process into manageable steps, helping to craft these important sections with accuracy and lucidity.

2.2 Writing the Background Section

Confirm that researchers have a profound understanding of the research problem or question that are addressing. Researchers should be capable of evidently expressing the gap in knowledge that the research plans to fill.

Carry out a systematic review of existing literature connected to the research topic. Identify key ideas, theories, and findings. This will help to place the research in the background of earlier work and exhibit consciousness of related studies.

State the gap or absence in the existing literature. What question or issue has not been sufficiently addressed? Describe why this gap is important and why it is worth studying.

Describe why the research is essential. What are the possible practical implications, theoretical contributions, or societal benefits of the study? How will it go forward knowledge in the field? Create a compelling case for why the research matters.

If the research topic has a historical aspect, briefly give historical background to help readers understand how the topic has changed over time. This can be particularly imperative in social science.

Examine the broader consequence of the research within the field. How does it contribute to the overall perception of the topic? What might it indicate for future research and policy decisions?

If the research involves particular terminology or concepts, define them unmistakably. Make sure that the readers have a concrete base for understanding the study.

If the research includes specific goals or hypotheses, briefly shape them in this section. However, keep them to the point; it will elaborate in the methodology and introduction sections.

The background section should be well-structured and flow logically. Use lucid and succinct language. Break down multifaceted ideas into digestible parts. It should normally be a few paragraphs to a few pages, depending on the difficulty of the topic and the length of the research.

Throughout the background section, cite the pertinent literature that has been reviewed. Appropriately format the citations consistent with the citation style required by the foundation or journal.

Make sure that the ideas are well-articulated and that there are no typos or errors.

2.3 Writing the Problem Statement

Before writing a problem statement, a deep understanding of the research area is essential. Perform a meticulous literature review to become conversant in the existing research, arguments, and gaps in knowledge associated with the topic.

The problem statement should start by identifying the exact gap or problem in the existing literature. What is absent or not well-understood? What question or subject requires further investigation or clarification? Be accurate and unambiguous in defining the gap.

The problem statement should be lucid, succinct, and concise. Avoid unclear or excessively broad statements that lack focus. Shape the problem in a single, well-articulated sentence or a short paragraph.

Use accurate and unambiguous language to explain the problem. Avoid jargon or technical terms that may not be well-known to all readers. Ensure that anyone with a fundamental understanding of the field can understand the problem statement.

Describe why this problem is important. What are the repercussions of not addressing it? How does solving this problem add to the field or have broader repercussions? Articulate the significance of the research.

If the research includes specific research questions or objectives, mention in brief them in the problem statement. This helps readers recognize how the study proposes to address the identified problem.

Be cautious not to suggest possible solutions in the problem statement. The objective is to describe the problem, not to suggest solutions. Set aside the argument of solutions for the methodology and discussion sections.

Reference-related studies or literature that holds up the existence of the problem. Demonstrate how the problem statement is grounded in earlier research and why it is a logical expansion of existing knowledge.

Make sure that the problem that is defined is within the scope of the research and that it is reasonable to investigate. It should be a problem that the researcher can logically address with the available resources and time.

The problem statement is an important part of the research, therefore take the time to modify and refine it. Seek advice from colleagues, supervisors, or advisors to certify lucidity and precision.

The problem statement is normally found in the introduction section, after the background, and before the methodology. It should logically flow from the background information.

Proofread the problem statement for grammatical and stylistic errors to make sure that it is well-written as well as easy to understand.

2.4 Writing the Motivation of the Study

Introduce the common research area or topic that the study deals with. Give several situations and background information to provide the reader with a clear perceptive of the subject matter.

Recognize an exact gap, problem, or unanswered issue in the current state of knowledge within the research area. This should be something that the research aims to tackle or contribute to. The gap or problem is what makes the need for the study.

Describe why this gap or problem is important. Thrash out the possible implications, results, or benefits of addressing this gap. Think about both the academic significance and the real-world consequence of the research.

Support the argument by referencing appropriate literature, studies, or preceding research that emphasizes the significance of the identified problem or gap. This demonstrates that the research is built upon existing knowledge and contributes to the incomplete scholarly conversation.

State the research questions or goals. These should unswervingly address the gap or identified problem. This helps readers recognize the exact goals of the study.

State any distinctive aspects of the study that set it apart from earlier research. Discuss why the approach, methodology, or data may suggest fresh insights or elucidations to the identified problem.

Explain how the research connects to broader themes, trends, or arguments in the field or connected fields. This shows the wider significance of the work.

Shape the motivation of the target audience. If researchers are writing for a specialized academic audience, employ suitable terminology and outline the significance within the framework of the field. If the audience includes non-specialists, give more background and circumstances.

Inscribe in a lucid, succinct, and engaging approach. Avoid jargon or excessively technical language that might isolate readers.

The motivation of the study is a decisive part of the introduction. Revise and improve it as needed to make sure that it efficiently expresses the implication of the research.

2.5 Writing the Rationale of the Study

State the overall intention of the research. What is the major objective of the study? This should be brief and expressed.

Describe the exact gap or lack in the existing literature that the research aims to deal with. Thrash out the limitations or gaps in earlier studies that make the research obligatory. Be precise about what has not been satisfactorily explored or unspoken.

Explain the broader implication of the research within the field. Discuss how the study contributes to advancing knowledge, solving practical problems, or addressing theoretical arguments. Why should others be concerned about the research? What influence could it have?

Depending on the nature of the research, highlight whether it has practical, theoretical, or policy relevance. Discuss how the findings could be applied in real-world conditions or how they contribute to theoretical arguments and perception.

Thrash out whether the timing of the research is important. Are there current events, trends, or developments that make the study mainly appropriate now? Describe why the research is well-timed and required at this point.

If the research aligns with broader goals, ideas, or plans in the field, state them. Elucidate how the study fits into larger research outlines.

Explain the possible benefits or inferences of the research, both within the academic community and from practical or policy perspectives. How might the findings change or perk up existing practices, policies, or perceptive?

Be exact and avoid using common phrases like "to advance knowledge" or "to contribute to the field." Instead, give real causes and examples that demonstrate why the research is important.

Reference-related studies or literature that supports the rationale. Explain how the research is grounded in the existing body of knowledge and why it is a rational expansion of earlier research work.

Consider the target audience when writing the rationale. Shape the explanation to suit the interests and apprehensions of the readers, whether they are specialists in the field or a broader audience.

While giving a wide-ranging rationale is significant, be aware of length. The rationale should be lucid and succinct, avoiding needless explanation.

Make sure that the points are well-articulated and there are no grammatical or typographical errors.

2.6 Writing the Significance of the Study

State the importance of the study briefly and simply. Make it apparent why the research matters.

Discuss how the research fits within the background of the broader pasture. Highlight how it addresses significant questions, matters, or gaps in existing knowledge.

If the research has practical submissions, explain how the findings could be applied in real-world conditions. Discuss how they might inform or perk up practices, policies, or decision-making practices.

If the research has theoretical implications, illustrate how it contributes to the theoretical outline of the field. Does it challenge existing theories, suggest new ideas, or refine existing models?

Think about the broader societal or cultural implications of the research. How might the findings impact public perceptions, behaviors, or attitudes? Explain any possible societal benefits or effects.

If the research introduces novel methods, technologies, or approaches, describe their implication and possible impact on future research in the field.

Connect the research to earlier studies or literature. Discuss how the research work builds upon or expands existing research and why it symbolizes an important development.

Explain the possible long-term influences of the research. Will the findings continue to be appropriate in the future? How might they form the direction of research in a particular area?

If the research has inferences for policy-making, discuss how it might inform policy decisions and contribute to solving real-world challenges.

Discuss what makes the study exceptional or innovative. Is it the research methodology, the focus on an understudied population, or an original standpoint? Make it clear why the study stands out.

Shape the justification of implication to the target audience. Think about whether the readers are experts in the field or a broader audience and adjust the language and examples accordingly.

While it's significant to express the implication of the study methodically, keep the explanation succinct and avoid needless jargon or complexity.

Ensure lucidity and logic. Eliminate any redundancies or ambiguities.

2.7 Writing the Broad Aims of the Study

State the broad aims of the study in an apparent and simple manner. Employ short language to explain the primary goals of the research.

Make sure that the broad aims are precise, definite, and quantifiable. Avoid unclear or excessively broad statements that lack focus. Each aim should be specific and feasible within the scope of the research.

Frame the broad aims using action verbs like investigate, examine, analyze, evaluate, or compare to articulate what the researcher proposes to do in the study.

The broad aims should directly relate to the research problem or questions which introduced in the introduction. Reveal how the broad aims tackle the identified problem or gap in the literature.

Ensure the broad aims are written in language that is reachable to a broad audience including those who may not be experts in the field. Avoid too many technical terms.

If the study has multiple aims, prioritize them in terms of their significance and importance to the research. Present the most decisive aims first and then move to secondary or supporting aims.

While it is necessary to be wide-ranging, avoid irresistible readers with too many aims. Restrict the number of aims to a manageable few to keep lucidity and focus.

Make sure that the aims are sensible and achievable within the constraints of the research project including time resources and access to data.

Talk about the expected outcomes or results related to each aim. This helps readers comprehend the reason and possible contributions of the study.

If the research is novel or offers a significant contribution to the field, reveal this when introducing the aims. Describe how the study goes beyond existing work.

While it is satisfactory to reiterate the aims for importance, avoid repeating them excessively throughout the introduction section. Point out them once obviously and then refer back to them as required.

After writing the aims of the study, proofread them carefully to ensure they are free of grammatical errors and uphold stability in wording and formatting.

On the whole, the aims of the study are placed towards the end of the introduction section, just before or after the research problem and the rationale of the study.

2.8 Writing the Literature Review

Consider the target audiences which are usually scholars and researchers in the field. Understand the reason for the literature review, which is to provide context, demonstrate the knowledge of the existing literature, and justify the need for the research.

Before start writing, make an outline that includes the key sections that plan to cover. Refer to the literature review format and give an overview of the organization and structure of the review.

Start with a clear and concise introduction that sets the stage for your literature review. State the research question or objective of the study and explain how the literature review contributes to addressing it. Outline the criteria researchers want to select the literature for the review. This could include factors like publication date, study design, geographic focus, or language. Justify the criteria and explain why included or excluded certain sources.

Organize the literature logically, by and large thematically or chronologically, depending on the research question. For each theme or topic, introduce it with a clear topic sentence that relates it to the research question.

For each source of consideration, provide a concise summary of its key findings, methodology, and major arguments. Make sure to cite each source properly using the citation style required for the paper. Summarize the main findings and insights from your literature review. Reiterate the importance of the research question and how the work contributes to the field. Suggest avenues for future research and any unresolved questions or contradictions in the literature.

Analyze and evaluate each source critically. Discuss its strengths, weaknesses, limitations, and relevance to your research. Synthesize the information by identifying trends, patterns, and gaps in the literature.

Connect the literature to the research question and explain how each source contributes to the understanding of the topic. Highlight any theoretical frameworks or models used in the literature.

Use transition sentences to smoothly guide the reader from one point or source to the next. This helps maintain a coherent flow.

Write in a formal and objective tone. Avoid personal opinions and biased language. Use academic language and avoid casual or informal terms.

Summarize the main points from each theme or subsection and reiterate their relevance to the research.

Connect different themes or subsections by discussing their interrelations and how they collectively address the research question.

In the final paragraphs, summarize the main findings, trends, and gaps in the literature. Emphasize the importance of the research in addressing these gaps.

Use a transitional sentence to smoothly transition from the literature review to the next section of the research paper.

Carefully edit and proofread the literature review to ensure clarity, coherence, and proper grammar. Check that the citations and references are accurate and adhere to the selected citation style.

2.9 Writing about the Research Gap

Summarize the key findings and insights from the literature review. Then, unambiguously state the research gap or gaps that have been identified based on the review of the existing literature. The gap should be a specific area or question that has not been adequately addressed or remains unanswered by earlier research.

Explain why this research gap is significant. What are the implications of this gap for the field or practical applications? Discuss how addressing this gap can contribute to the advancement of knowledge in the area of study.

Connect the identified research gap to the research question or objective. Explain how the study aims to fill this gap. State how the research will address or contribute to resolving the identified gap.

Provide evidence and reasoning for why the gap exists. Researchers can refer to limitations in previous studies, changes in the field, emerging trends, or evolving technologies. Support the justification with citations from the literature reviewed.

Emphasize the novelty of the research. Explain why the study is different from earlier work and why it is uniquely positioned to address the gap. Describe the potential contribution the research can make to the field. What new insights, methods, or solutions will it offer?

Be clear and concise in the description of the research gap. Avoid unnecessary jargon or complexity.

Conclude the discussion of the research gap by smoothly transitioning to the next section of the research paper, which is typically the research proposal or methodology section. Use a transitional sentence to indicate how the study will deal with the identified gap.

When researchers start discussing the research proposal, revisit the research gap and elaborate on how the study's methodology, design, and objectives will specifically target this gap.

Before finalizing the literature review section, proofread and revise the discussion of the research gap to ensure clarity and coherence.

2.10 Types of Literature Review

1. Narrative Literature Review

This is the most common type of literature review and gives a widespread summary and synthesis of the existing literature on a specific topic. It follows a narrative structure, presenting the literature in a logical and organized manner without an exact quantitative analysis. The objective is to give a broad overview of the topic and identify key themes, trends, and gaps in the literature.

2. Systematic Literature Review

A systematic review follows a structured and thorough process to systematically look for, select, and crucially review pertinent studies. It often includes a meta-analysis, which quantitatively combines the results of selected studies to draw statistically significant conclusions. Systematic reviews aim to reduce bias and subjectivity in the review process.

3. Meta-Analysis Literature Review

While technically not a literature review, a meta-analysis is often associated with systematic reviews. It involves statistical analysis to combine and synthesize the results of multiple studies on a particular topic, providing a quantitative summary of the evidence. Meta-analyses are valuable for determining the overall effect size and significance of an intervention or relationship.

4. Scoping Literature Review

Scoping reviews aim to map the existing literature on a broad topic or research area. They provide an overview of the main concepts, key sources, and gaps in the literature without necessarily conducting a detailed critical appraisal of individual studies. Scoping reviews are helpful when the literature on a topic is extensive and heterogeneous.

5. Critical Literature Review

This type of review focuses on critically evaluating and analyzing the strengths and weaknesses of existing research. It often involves a thorough critique of the methodologies, theoretical frameworks, and conclusions of individual studies. The objective is to identify areas where future research is required and to measure the reliability and validity of existing findings.

6. Integrative Literature Review

Integrative reviews go beyond summarizing the literature by synthesizing information from various sources and disciplines. They plan to give a holistic understanding of a complex topic, often involving a synthesis of qualitative and quantitative data.

7. Historical Literature Review

Historical reviews examine the development of a particular topic or field of research over time. They trace the evolution of ideas, theories, and methodologies in the literature, highlighting key milestones and changes.

8. Theoretical Literature Review

Theoretical reviews focus on examining the theoretical frameworks and concepts that have been used in the literature on a specific topic. They explore how different theories have been applied and developed in various studies and their implications for future research.

9. Methodological Literature Review

Methodological reviews focus on the research methods and approaches employed in previous studies. They assess the strengths and limitations of different research methods and guide the most appropriate methods for future research.

2.11 Narrative Literature Review

This is used:

When researchers want to explore a topic that has not been extensively researched, a narrative literature review can provide a broad understanding of the existing knowledge and help identify areas where further investigation is needed.

In the early stages of a research study, a narrative review can serve as a foundational step to familiarize with the key concepts, theories, and empirical studies related to the research area.

When the research topic is broad or interdisciplinary, a narrative review allows for covering a wide range of relevant literature and providing readers with a holistic view of the subject.

If the research involves examining the historical development of a concept, theory, or field, a narrative review can trace the evolution of ideas over time.

Narrative reviews are effective in identifying trends, patterns, and gaps in the literature. Researchers can highlight the dominant themes, controversies, or unreciprocated questions in the field.

When researchers are developing a conceptual framework or theoretical foundation for their research, a narrative review can help them understand the existing theories and concepts in the area of study.

If the research aim is to inform policy or practice, a narrative review can summarize the relevant research findings and their implications for decision-makers.

From an educational perspective, narrative literature reviews are often used to teach students about a specific topic, providing them with a comprehensive understanding of the subject matter.

When conducting a systematic review or meta-analysis would be resource-intensive or impractical due to time or resource constraints, a narrative review can be a more feasible option to summarize existing knowledge.

In qualitative research, narrative reviews can help situate the study within the broader context of existing qualitative research on the topic.

2.12 Systematic Literature Review

This is used:

When researchers need to answer specific research questions or hypotheses by systematically summarizing and synthesizing all available evidence on an exacting topic.

For difficult or controversial topics a clear and unbiased synthesis of evidence is required to resolve debates or uncertainties.

Researchers want to minimize bias in the literature review process by following a structured and transparent methodology, which helps reduce subjectivity and ensure reproducibility.

When researchers plan to conduct a quantitative meta-analysis to statistically combine and analyze the results of multiple studies, it provides a more precise estimate of the overall effect size.

Researchers aim to compare different interventions, treatments, or approaches to determine which one is most efficient or correct.

When developing policy recommendations or systematic assessments of environmental or social factors, systematic reviews are used to inform the decision-making process.

When researchers want to adhere to a structured and transparent methodology that includes predefined criteria for study selection, data extraction, and quality assessment.

Systematic reviews can be used to synthesize and evaluate the effectiveness of educational interventions and teaching methods in educational research.

Systematic reviews are used to assess the impact of environmental factors or interventions on ecosystems, species, or natural resources in environmental sciences.

2.13 Meta-analysis Literature Review

This is used:

When the research question involves quantitatively summarizing the results of multiple studies to calculate an overall effect size or estimate the magnitude and direction of an effect.

To increase the precision and reliability of the findings by pooling data from multiple studies to obtain a more accurate estimate of the effect size.

To compare the effectiveness of different interventions, treatments, or approaches, meta-analysis allows for quantitatively assessing and comparing their outcomes.

To explore and quantify sources of heterogeneity (variability) in study results by conducting subgroup analyses or meta-regression.

In circumstances where the literature contains conflicting or inconclusive results, a meta-analysis can help resolve these discrepancies and give a more perfect conclusion.

To assess and correct for publication bias, which occurs when only studies with significant results are published, leading to an overestimation of effect sizes.

If researchers are interested in understanding how study quality and participant characteristics influence the effect size or outcomes, meta-analysis allows analyzing these moderator variables quantitatively.

In fields where research outcomes are typically quantitative (effect sizes, mean differences, odds ratios), meta-analysis is an important tool for synthesizing and summarizing these data.

In fields where research on a specific topic accumulates over time, meta-analysis helps produce a growing body of evidence, incorporating new studies into the analysis.

To estimate the overall effect of a treatment or intervention across diverse populations, settings, or conditions.

2.14 Scoping literature review

This is used:

To gain a preliminary understanding of a research area that has not been comprehensively studied or when the topic is relatively new and emerging.

To define and refine the scope of the research, identify key concepts and themes as well as develop research questions.

To identify the range of literature and subdomains within the broader topic when the research areas are multifaceted, interdisciplinary, or have diverse subtopics.

Before conducting a systematic review or meta-analysis, a scoping review can help determine whether there is sufficient related literature to deserve a more comprehensive review.

To identify gaps in the existing literature, including areas where research is lacking or where further inquiry is required.

To give an overview of the extent, nature, and distribution of research literature on a specific topic or research question.

In social sciences and humanities, scoping reviews are important for exploring and synthesizing diverse perspectives, theories, and methodologies related to a research topic.

When the literature includes not only empirical research studies but also theoretical papers, conceptual frameworks, expert opinions, or other non-empirical sources.

To understand how research on a specific topic has evolved and to trace the development of ideas and theories.

As part of the primary steps in research project planning, a scoping review can help define research objectives, develop search strategies, and identify pertinent sources and databases.

2.15 Critical Literature Review

This is used:

To assess the quality and rigor of the research methodologies used in previous studies, including their sampling, data collection, and analysis methods.

To determine the validity and reliability of the findings in the literature, particularly when examining the potential for bias, confounding variables, or limitations in study design.

To examine and assess the theoretical frameworks, models, or conceptual frameworks used in the literature, evaluating their correctness and applicability to the research background.

To detect and discuss potential biases in the literature, including publication bias, reporting bias, and researcher bias as well as their implications for the overall conclusions.

To assess the representativeness of the study samples in the literature and consider whether they sufficiently reflect the population or context of interest.

To analyze the data collection methods used in earlier studies, including surveys, interviews, observations, or experiments, and their possible impact on the findings.

To evaluate the generalizability of research findings to different populations, settings, or situations and consider the external validity of the studies.

To assess the appropriateness and robustness of statistical analyses, including the choice of statistical tests, assumptions, and statistical power.

To identify and analyze the sources of disagreement and potential explanations when there are conflicting or contradictory findings in the literature.

To evaluate the theoretical contributions and scholarly debates in the literature, including the strengths and weaknesses of different theoretical perspectives.

To identify areas where research is lacking or where further investigation is essential based on limitations and gaps identified in existing studies.

To provide a balanced assessment of the evidence when the research topic is multifaceted, controversial, or subject to conflicting interpretations.

2.16 Integrative Literature Review

This is used:

When the research topic is comprehensive, interdisciplinary, or covers a range of perspectives, theories, or methodologies from various disciplines or subfields.

To gather research studies that use different research methods to tackle different aspects of a research question.

In interdisciplinary research contexts, it is significant to bridge gaps between different fields of study and combine insights from numerous disciplines.

To synthesize and integrate various theoretical frameworks, models, or conceptual perspectives that have been applied in the literature.

To provide readers with a widespread and holistic perceptive of a multifaceted research topic, taking into account various dimensions, factors, and contexts.

In areas of research that are comparatively new or rapidly evolving, an integrative literature review can help secure and make sense of a mounting body of literature.

To explore and compare diverse perceptions, perspectives, and theories related to a research topic.

To identify and analyze patterns, trends, and commonalities across different studies and perspectives in the literature.

In situations where the literature encloses conflicting findings or interpretations, an integrative review can help elucidate these discrepancies by considering diverse angles.

To generate new insights, theories, or conceptual frameworks by synthesizing and integrating existing knowledge.

In situations where the synthesis of different evidence is essential for policy development, decision-making, or practice guidelines.

To trace the cumulative development of knowledge on a research topic over time, including how ideas, theories, and research methodologies have evolved.

2.17 Historical Literature Review

This is used:

To trace the historical development of key ideas, theories, or concepts within a specific research area to understand their origins, evolution, and influences.

To give historical context and perspective to current research, theories, or practices in a field by examining their historical roots and antecedents.

To emphasize important historical milestones, penetrates, or seminal works that have shaped the development of a research topic.

To explore the academic lines and influences of researchers, scholars, or theorists who have contributed to a particular field.

To examine the history of paradigm shifts, changes in theoretical frameworks, or shifts in research methodologies within a field.

To understand how research methods and methodologies have evolved and how they have been applied within a research area.

To analyze historical debates, controversies, or disagreements within a field and how these debates have influenced the development of ideas.

To trace the historical evolution of research ethics, regulations, and ethical reflections within a discipline.

To revisit and re-evaluate past research, theories, or practices in light of current knowledge and to assess their relevance and implications for current research.

To observe when historical events, social changes, or cultural shifts have had a significant impact on the development of a research topic.

2.18 Theoretical Literature Review

This is used:

To clarify and define key concepts, terms, or constructs pertinent to the research topic, ensuring a solid theoretical foundation for the study.

In the premature stages of research planning, a theoretical review can help to develop a theoretical framework or conceptual model to guide the research design and data analysis.

To evaluate and assess the strengths and weaknesses of existing theories and theoretical perspectives within a particular research field.

To identify gaps in existing theoretical frameworks, models, or concepts and highlight areas where new theoretical contributions are needed.

To synthesize and integrate multiple theoretical perspectives, paradigms, or schools of thought that have been applied to a research topic, providing a more holistic view.

To compare and contrast different theoretical approaches or paradigms within a field to identify their commonalities, differences, and implications.

To motivate theoretical innovation by exploring how existing theories and concepts can be extended, refined, or adapted to address new research questions or emerging trends.

To inform the research design by selecting suitable theoretical frameworks and concepts that aligns with the research objectives and hypotheses.

To understand a phenomenon or make predictions where the research is theory-driven, meaning that researchers are explicitly testing or applying theoretical concepts.

To explore the historical development of theoretical frameworks or models within a field to understand their evolution and influences.

2.19 Methodological Literature Review

This is used:

To select a proper research design, data collection methods, or analytical approaches for the research study, a methodological review can help to evaluate and compare different options.

In the early stages of research planning, a methodological review can help in developing a methodological framework or research methodology that aligns with the research objectives.

To evaluate and assess the strengths and limitations of research methods and methodologies employed in earlier studies within a particular research pasture.

To identify gaps in existing research methods, methodologies, or approaches and find out areas where new methodological contributions are required.

To synthesize and integrate multiple research methods or methodological approaches that has been applied to a research topic, providing a comprehensive view of the available approaches.

To compare and contrast diverse methodological approaches, their applicability, and their implications for research results.

To motivate methodological innovation by exploring how existing research methods and methodologies can be extended, adapted, or refined to deal with new research questions or emerging trends.

To examine how the preference of research methods and methodologies has influenced the findings and interpretations of earlier studies within a field.

In cases where the research aims to align with or replicate the research methods used in previous studies to develop or confirm previous findings.

2.20 Empirical Literature Review

This is used:

To create and sum up the empirical research findings from multiple studies to answer a particular research question or hypothesis.

To identify and analyze trends, patterns, and commonalities in empirical research within a specific ground or research topic.

To evaluate the quality, rigidity, and methodological approaches used in earlier empirical studies including their research design, sampling, data collection, and analysis methods.

To identify gaps in the existing empirical research, highlighting areas where further empirical examinations are required.

To measure the strength and robustness of the empirical evidence supporting particular hypotheses, theories, or research arguments.

To compare and distinguish the results and conclusions of various empirical studies to make out areas of agreement, disagreement, or contradiction.

Evidence-based decision-making relies on a meticulous review of empirical research findings.

To analyze the results of multiple empirical studies through meta-analysis or other statistical methods.

To create the cumulative knowledge and research findings on a particular topic over time, tracing the expansion of empirical research within a field.

In circumstances where the empirical research findings behind policies, practices, or interferences are significant for informed decision-making and development.

To scrutinize the historical development of empirical research on a particular topic, tracking changes in research methodologies and findings.

3. Writing the Theoretical Framework

3.1 Introduction

A theoretical framework offers a conceptual foundation for the study. It helps to define key concepts, variables, and relationships between them. Without a theoretical framework, research can lack structure and consistency. It helps in the formulation of research questions or hypotheses. By grounding the study in existing theories or models, researchers can identify gaps in knowledge or areas where further investigation is required. A strong theoretical framework reveals scholarly rigor and depth of study. It demonstrates that the study is not just a collection of facts but is rooted in established theory and methodology. A theoretical framework is indispensable because it shapes the whole research process, from formulating research questions to analyzing data and drawing conclusions. This chapter guides how the theoretical framework should be presented.

3.2 Writing the Theoretical Framework

Make sure that there is a clear understanding of the research topic, research questions, and objectives. Researchers should also have conducted a thorough literature review to recognize related theories and concepts.

Make out the key theories, models, and concepts that are pertinent to the research. These should be the theories that will guide the analysis and help answer the research questions.

Define and explain the key terms and concepts used in the theoretical framework. This is crucial to make sure that readers understand the terminology that will be used throughout the study.

Give an overview of the theoretical perspective that supports the research. Explain the school of thought or paradigm that the study aligns with. For instance, in the case of a sociological study, a researcher might discuss whether the research is rooted in functionalism, conflict theory, or figurative interactionism.

Sum up and discuss the pertinent literature that supports the selected theoretical framework. Explain how earlier research has informed the selection and understanding of the theoretical perspective.

Create a conceptual model or diagram that visually represents the relationships between the key variables or concepts in the research. This can help readers grasp the theoretical framework more easily.

Give a rationale for why have selected this particular theoretical framework. Explain how it is the most appropriate for addressing the research questions and how it fills gaps in the existing literature.

Admit any assumptions that motivate the theoretical framework. Be transparent about the limitations or potential biases associated with the selected viewpoint.

Coherent how the theoretical framework relates to the research questions. Show how the framework will guide the data collection, examination, and interpretation.

If the research includes hypotheses or propositions, explain how they are derived from or linked to the theoretical framework. This demonstrates the practical application of the selected theory.

Conclude the theoretical framework section by summarizing the key points and concepts. Emphasize the importance of the selected framework in shaping the direction and focus of the study.

Re-examine the theoretical framework section to ensure lucidity, logic, and logical flow.

3.3 Components of a Theoretical Framework

Introduce the topic and context of the research. Explain why the study is important and provide a brief overview of the problem or research question aimed to address.

Recognize and define the key concepts and variables that the research study will focus on. Clearly explain what these terms mean and their relevance to the study.

Select a theoretical perspective or framework that aligns with the research. This could be a particular theory, model, or paradigm that provides a lens through which to analyze the topic. For example, if the researcher is studying consumer behavior, a researcher might select the Theory of Planned Behaviour.

Give a succinct summary of the existing literature related to the topic and the selected theoretical perspective. Highlight key studies, theories, and concepts that support the approach. Explain how these earlier works inform the understanding of the problem.

If the theoretical framework relies on specific assumptions or theoretical propositions, articulate them clearly. These assumptions and propositions form the basis for the research hypotheses.

Describe the relationships between the key variables or concepts in the study. Use text, diagrams, or models to illustrate these relationships if it enhances clarity. Show how the theoretical framework provides a structure for understanding these relationships.

Describe why this particular theoretical framework was selected. Discuss how it is well-suited to address the research question or problem. Highlight the advantages of using this framework over other possible alternatives.

Connect the theoretical framework to the research questions or objectives. Explain how the framework will guide the research process including data collection, examination, and interpretation.

Be transparent about any limitations or potential biases associated with the selected theoretical framework. Recognize that no framework is perfect and address how the plan will reduce these limitations.

Wrap up the section by summarizing the fundamental elements of the theoretical framework. Provide a clear and concise overview of the key concepts, theoretical perspective, and identified relationships.

Depending on the structure of the research study, researchers can use the end of the theoretical framework section to transition smoothly into the methodology section. Explain how the selected framework informs the research design and data collection methods.

Review the theoretical framework section for clarity, coherence, and consistency. Ensure that it logically flows from one point to the next, providing a clear foundation for the study.

3.4 Selecting the Most Relevant Theories and Concepts

Comprehensively understanding the research topic and the specific research question or problem that aims to address. Clearly define the scope and boundaries of the study.

Start with a comprehensive literature review. Search for scholarly articles, books, reports, and other relevant sources related to the topic. Use academic databases like Scopus, PubMed, Google Scholar, JSTOR, or the institution's library resources.

Develop a list of keywords and search terms related to the research topic. Use these terms when searching for literature and experiment with diverse combinations of keywords to cast a wide net.

As researchers collect sources, categorize and organize them based on the theories, concepts, and themes they discuss. This can help to identify recurring ideas and patterns in the literature.

Concentrate on any theories, models, or frameworks that are frequently cited or discussed in the literature. These are likely to be key theories relevant to the research topic.

Some research papers may present conceptual frameworks that illustrate the relationships between key concepts in a particular field. These frameworks can be valuable in identifying important concepts.

Review the reference lists and citations of the articles. If multiple sources cite the same theory or concept, it's a strong indication of its importance within the field.

Look for guidance from supervisors, professors, advisors, or experts in a particular field. They can provide valuable insights into the most relevant theories and concepts for the study.

Analyze the historical development of the research area. Understanding how theories and concepts have evolved can help to identify foundational ideas.

Assess the relevance of each theory or concept to the specific research question. Some theories may be more directly applicable, while others may provide background context.

Think about the robustness and empirical support for the related theories and concepts. Are they well-established and widely accepted in the field, or are they more speculative?

Evaluate how well each theory or concept aligns with the research objectives and the chosen hypotheses to test. Choose the ones that provide the most suitable framework for the study.

Based on the evaluations, create a shortlist of the key theories and concepts that plan to be incorporated into the research study.

Provide a clear justification for why researchers have selected specific theories and concepts. Explain how they contribute to the theoretical foundation of the study.

Remain open to revising the selection of theories and concepts if researchers find new evidence or standpoints that permit a change.

3.6 Defining Key Terms and Concepts

List the key terms and concepts relevant to the study. These are usually the central ideas, variables, or constructs that the study revolves around. Ensure the central ideas, variables or constructs have been identified through the literature review and research question development.

For each key term or concept, give a succinct and clear definition. Employ precise language to explain what each term means within the context of the study. If a term has multiple meanings, spell out the definition that will be used in the research.

Whenever feasible, depend on established and recognized definitions from reputable sources, for example, academic journals, dictionaries, or authoritative texts. Cite these sources to lend trustworthiness to the definitions.

Be attentive to avoiding vagueness and ambiguity in the definitions. Ensure that there is no room for misinterpretation or misunderstanding regarding the meaning of key terms.

Keep the target audience in mind when defining terms. If the research paper is intended for a specialized audience familiar with the field, the researcher may use technical definitions. However, if the paper is for a broader audience, use language that is accessible to non-specialists.

To improve understanding, consider including examples or scenarios that illustrate how each key term or concept is applied in practice. This can help readers grasp the real-world implications of the definitions.

If there are multifaceted interrelationships between key terms or concepts, briefly describe these connections in the definitions. This can help readers see how these terms fit into the broader framework of the research.

It is essential to give additional contextual information along with the definitions. Explain why these terms are relevant to the research and how they contribute to addressing the research question.

Make sure consistency in your use of terms throughout the research paper. Employ similar definitions and terminology consistently in the introduction, theoretical framework, methodology, results, and discussion sections.

If researchers are using acronyms or abbreviations for key terms or concepts, spell them out and give the full definition the first time the researcher uses them in the study. Afterward, researchers can use the acronym or abbreviation as shorthand.

Review the definitions for lucidity and succinctness. Look for reactions from peers and supervisors to ensure that the definitions are efficient and understandable.

Place the definitions of key terms and concepts within the theoretical framework section of the research study. This ensures that readers have a clear understanding of the foundational concepts before delving into the rest of the study.

3.7 Explaining the Theoretical Standpoint

State the theoretical perspective that is adopted or the theoretical framework researchers are using. Explain the broader philosophical or intellectual tradition it belongs to.

Recommend a concise overview of the core principles, ideas, and assumptions of the theoretical perspective. Highlight its main concepts and themes. This helps readers unfamiliar with the standpoint recognize its fundamentals.

Give a historical context by discussing the origins of the theoretical perspective and the thinkers or scholars who have significantly contributed to its development. Explain how previous ideas have influenced the viewpoint.

Identify and define the key theoretical concepts or constructs associated with the perspective. Explain what these terms mean within the context of the study and how they relate to the research question.

Discuss the underlying assumptions or premises of the theoretical perspective. Explain the worldview it represents and the fundamental beliefs that shape its approach to understanding the world.

Explain why researchers have selected this particular theoretical perspective for the study. Discuss how it aligns with the research question, objectives, and the phenomena that aim to investigate. Highlight its suitability in addressing the research goals.

If appropriate, briefly compare and contrast the selected theoretical perspective with alternative perspectives or theories within a similar field. Explain why researchers have opted for one over the others and how it offers exclusive insights.

Show how the theoretical perspective is situated within the existing body of literature related to your research topic. Discuss how it builds upon or challenges previous theories and contributes to the ongoing scholarly discourse.

Use real examples or case studies to illustrate how the theoretical perspective has been applied in earlier research or how it can be applied to the specific research background.

Discuss the practical and theoretical implications of adopting this perspective. Explain how it guides the research methodology, data analysis, and interpretation of results.

Recognize any limitations or criticisms associated with the theoretical perspective. Be transparent about potential weaknesses or areas where the perspective may not fully explain the phenomena researchers are studying.

Conclude the explanation of the theoretical perspective by emphasizing its importance in shaping the theoretical framework of the research. Highlight how it serves as a foundational lens through which the study is conducted.

Ensure that the explanation is clear, concise, and well-structured. Avoid overly technical or jargon-heavy language that might be difficult for the readers to understand.

Review the explanation of the theoretical perspective after getting advice from peers and supervisors.

3.8 Discussing the Related Literature that Supports the Selected Theoretical Framework

Organize the literature that supports the theoretical framework. Group relevant sources and studies together based on the theories, concepts, or perspectives they focus on. This will help to present a logical debate.

Start the argument with the foundational or seminal works that have shaped the selected theoretical framework. Identify the key scholars, theories, or models that are the keystones of the viewpoint.

Review the key concepts, principles, or assumptions presented in the foundational literature. Provide clear and concise explanations of these concepts, highlighting their significance to the research.

Discuss how the theoretical framework has evolved. Identify significant developments, refinements, or modifications made by subsequent researchers. Show how the framework has adapted to new challenges.

Present empirical evidence or studies that have used the theoretical framework effectively. Explain how these studies have tested or applied the framework to real-world situations. Include examples of research findings that support the framework's validity.

Admit any variations or sub-schools of thought within the selected theoretical framework. Discuss any ongoing debates or controversies in the field connected to the framework. This reveals a nuanced understanding of the theory.

Compare and contrast the selected theoretical framework with alternative frameworks or theories in your field. Explain why chose one over the others and how it provides a better fit for the study.

Continuously connect the literature discussion to the specific research question or problem. Explain how the concepts and ideas from the literature are relevant to addressing the research objectives.

Demonstrate how the selected theoretical framework integrates and synthesizes different concepts and ideas from the literature. Highlight the framework's ability to provide a comprehensive lens for understanding the research topic.

Address any gaps or limitations in the empirical research that support the theoretical framework. This can include areas where more research is needed or situations where the framework may not fully explain certain phenomena.

Make sure that the argument maintains continuity and consistency throughout. Avoid jumping between different concepts or theories without providing a clear narrative thread that ties them together.

Cite all the relevant literature researchers want to discuss in the theoretical framework. Pursue the citation style guidelines.

Keep the argument clear and concise, avoiding unnecessary jargon or overly technical language. Strive for clarity so that readers can easily follow the argument.

Conclude the literature discussion by summarizing the key points and how they collectively support the selected theoretical framework. Reiterate why this framework is essential for the research.

Review the literature discussion for clarity, coherence, and relevance.

3.9 Creating a Conceptual Model or Diagram

Identify the central variables or concepts that are crucial to the research study. These are the elements that the conceptual model will represent.

For each variable or concept, give a clear and concise definition. Label them with descriptive names or symbols. Use consistent terminology and notation throughout the diagram.

Analyze the relationships between the variables or concepts. Are they positively or negatively correlated? Is there a causal relationship? Are they moderating or mediating factors? Ensure that researchers have a clear understanding of how they interact.

Select an appropriate tool for creating the diagram. Researchers can use software applications or researchers can create hand-drawn diagrams if they are clear and legible.

Use the selected tool to create the diagram.

i. Place the most central variable or concept at the center of the diagram. This represents the main focus of the study.

ii. Use arrows or lines to connect the variables or concepts. Use directional arrows to indicate the direction of relationships ($\rightarrow$ for causality, $\leftrightarrow$ for correlation).

iii. Tag the arrows or lines to describe the nature of the relationship.

iv. Add brief descriptive text near each variable or concept to clarify its role or significance in the model. This text should provide context for readers.

e. Use shapes and colors to distinguish between different types of variables or concepts or to group related elements together.

Arrange the layout of the diagram to make sure it's visually appealing and easy to follow. Arrange elements in a logical order, with the central concept in the center and related concepts radiating outward.

Test the conceptual model with colleagues, advisors, or peers to ensure it effectively represents your theoretical framework. Incorporate feedback and make any necessary refinements to improve clarity and accuracy.

If the diagram involves complex symbols or color-coding, include a key that explains the meaning of each element.

Plan for simplicity and clarity in the diagram. Avoid overcrowding with too many variables or concepts and ensure that the relationships are easy to understand at a glance.

Insert the completed diagram into the research study, typically within the theoretical framework section. Provide a caption or brief explanation to guide readers on how to interpret the diagram.

If the study evolves or if researchers receive feedback suggesting improvements, be prepared to revise and update the conceptual model in the study accordingly.

3.10 Relevance and Significance of the Theoretical Preference

State the research questions or objectives. Be specific about what researchers aim to investigate or understand in the study. This provides context for explaining the relevance of the selected theoretical framework.

Bring in the theoretical framework researchers have selected and briefly summarize its core concepts and principles. Provide a concise overview of the framework to ensure the readers understand the basis of the preference.

Explain how the selected theoretical framework aligns with the research questions. Highlight the key concepts or variables within the framework that directly relate to the research objectives. Show how these concepts are a natural fit for the study.

Argue how earlier research within the field has used or applied the same theoretical framework or similar ones. Cite relevant studies that have explored similar research questions or phenomena using this framework.

Identify gaps or limitations in the existing literature that the selected theoretical framework can address. This could include gaps in understanding, unexplored relationships, or unanswered questions that the study seeks to fill.

Discuss the strengths and advantages of the theoretical framework. Explain why it is well-suited for the study. Consider factors such as its explanatory power, flexibility, or ability to accommodate various aspects of the study.

Mention any alternative theoretical frameworks researchers considered and explain why researchers selected the selected one over others. Highlight the unique contributions and advantages of the selected framework about the alternatives.

Give examples or scenarios that illustrate how the theoretical framework has been successfully applied to similar research questions or contexts. These examples can demonstrate its effectiveness.

Describe how the selected theoretical framework will guide the research methodology, data collection, analysis, and interpretation. Show how it provides a structured approach to answering the research questions.

Emphasize how the study, guided by this framework, contributes to the field's knowledge by addressing previously unexplored aspects or by offering a novel perspective on existing issues.

Be apparent about any potential limitations or challenges associated with the selected theoretical framework. Address concerns that might arise and explain how to mitigate them.

Wrap up this section by summarizing the significance of the selected theoretical framework in addressing the research questions and filling gaps in the literature. Emphasize the potential contributions the study will make to the field.

Make sure that the explanation is clear, concise, and focused. Avoid excessive jargon or technical language that may make it difficult for readers to grasp the importance of the preference.

3.11 Highlighting the Assumptions that Motivate the Theoretical Framework

State the theoretical framework researchers are using. This could be a particular theory, model, or perspective that guides the study.

List and explain the key assumptions that underlie the theoretical framework. These assumptions are often unspoken, so researchers will need to make them explicit for the readers. Consider what foundational beliefs or premises the theory or framework relies on.

Describe why these assumptions are necessary for the study. Discuss how they align with the research problem and objectives.

Admit that there might be alternative assumptions or theoretical frameworks that could be used for a similar research problem. Compare and contrast the assumptions of the selected framework with those of other relevant frameworks, explaining why researchers have selected or used it.

Give empirical or theoretical evidence that supports the validity of the assumptions. This can enhance the credibility of the selected framework.

Be transparent about the limitations of the assumptions. Discuss any uncertainties or criticisms associated with them.

Explain how these assumptions influence the research design, methodology, and interpretation of results. What are the implications of these assumptions for the study?

Make sure that the explanations and discussions are in a language that is easily understandable to the target audience including both experts and non-experts in the field.

Use concrete examples or scenarios to illustrate how these assumptions apply to the study. This can make them more relatable and tangible.

Encourage readers to critically engage with the assumptions. Invite them to question the validity of these assumptions or explore alternative perspectives.

At the time of progressing, revisit and reassess the assumptions. If new evidence or insights emerge, be open to adjusting the theoretical framework accordingly.

In the conclusion or summary, reiterate the key assumptions and their importance in shaping the study. Emphasize how they relate to the research's contributions and implications.

3.12 Relationship between Theoretical Framework and Research Questions

Theoretical frameworks give background for the research questions. They help to understand the existing knowledge, theories, and concepts relevant to the topic, allowing the formulation of more focused and informed research questions.

The theoretical framework can guide the formulation of the research questions. It influences the aspects of the topic that researchers want to investigate, the variables researchers want to measure and the relationships researchers aim to explore.

If the research involves hypotheses, the theoretical framework often informs the development of these hypotheses. It suggests the expected relationships between variables based on the theory or conceptual model researchers are using.

The theoretical framework helps to determine the data collection methods and analytical techniques. It may guide in selecting appropriate tools, surveys, or experiments to gather and analyze data in line with the research questions.

When obtaining research results, the theoretical framework gives a lens through which researchers interpret these findings. It helps to understand the implications of the results within the context of existing theory and research.

By referring to the theoretical framework, researchers can identify gaps in the existing literature and pinpoint where the research questions contribute new knowledge or challenge existing assumptions.

An appropriate theoretical framework can help to justify the research questions. It demonstrates that the questions are grounded in established theory and are not arbitrary or disconnected from existing knowledge.

A strong theoretical framework ensures that the research questions are logically connected and coherent. It helps prevent the study from becoming a collection of unrelated questions or variables.

The theoretical framework often leads researchers to relevant literature sources that can inform the research questions and provide background information for the study.

When conducting a literature review, the theoretical framework helps to identify and synthesize studies that are aligned with the theories and concepts that are used in the study.

3.13 Connecting Hypotheses to the Theoretical Framework

Before creating hypotheses, thoroughly understand the core concepts, principles, and assumptions of the theoretical framework. This deep understanding will help to formulate hypotheses that align with the framework.

Within the theoretical framework, identify the key concepts, variables, and relationships that are relevant to the study. These will serve as the foundation for the hypotheses.

Formulate hypotheses based on the concepts and relationships identified in the theoretical framework. Hypotheses should be clear, specific, and testable statements that express the expected relationships or outcomes in the study.

When crafting the hypotheses, use language and terminology consistent with the theoretical framework. This ensures that the hypotheses are in sync with the theoretical concepts and principles.

Provide a rationale for each hypothesis by explaining how it logically follows from the theoretical framework. Clarify why researchers expect the relationships or outcomes specified in the hypotheses based on the underlying theory.

Examine whether the hypotheses align with the broader theoretical framework. Check if there are any contradictions or inconsistencies between the hypotheses and the theory.

Acknowledge the possibility of alternative hypotheses that may contradict or challenge the theoretical framework. This demonstrates that researchers have considered multiple perspectives and helps make the study more robust.

Discuss how the hypotheses build upon or extend the existing theory. Emphasize the novel aspects of the research and how it advances the understanding of the theoretical concepts.

Cite previous research or evidence that supports the hypotheses researchers have formulated within the context of the theoretical framework. This strengthens the credibility of the hypotheses.

Specify the methods and data analysis techniques researchers will use to test the hypotheses derived from the theoretical framework. Make sure that the research design and data collection align with the hypotheses.

Make sure that the research design and data collection methods are designed to directly test the hypotheses, making the link between theory and empirical investigation explicit.

Throughout the research process, be open to revising the hypotheses if new information or findings emerge. Ensure to update them in a way that maintains alignment with the theoretical framework.

3.14 Summarizing the Theoretical Framework

Restate the theoretical framework researchers have used in the study. Clearly state the name of the theory, model, or perspective and provide a brief overview of its key elements.

Identify and emphasize the core concepts or variables within the theoretical framework. These are the fundamental building blocks of the study.

Summarize the critical relationships or hypotheses that are derived from the theoretical framework. Highlight any expected cause-and-effect relationships or patterns that the study will investigate.

Explain why the selected theoretical framework is relevant to the study. Discuss how it helps to address the research questions or objectives.

Show how the theoretical framework directly relates to and informs the research questions. Explain how it guided the formulation of the research questions.

Thrash out how the study contributes to the understanding of the theoretical framework. Mention any novel insights, extensions, or modifications researchers have made to the theory as a result of the study.

Remind the readers of the key assumptions that underlie the theoretical framework. Make it clear how these assumptions have influenced the research design and interpretation of results.

Acknowledge any limitations or criticisms associated with the theoretical framework. Be transparent about the framework's boundaries and its potential shortcomings.

Reflect on the broader implications of the theoretical framework for the study and the field as a whole. Consider how it contributes to theory development, practice, or policy.

Keep the summary concise and focused. Avoid unnecessary jargon or overly complex language. Aim for clarity and accessibility.

Encourage further research and exploration of the theoretical framework by highlighting areas where more investigation is needed or where your study leaves unanswered questions.

Connect the theoretical framework's summary to the overall significance of the study. Explain how a solid theoretical foundation strengthens the credibility and relevance of the study.

Wrap up the summary of the theoretical framework with a strong closing statement that reinforces the importance of the framework in guiding the study.

3.15 Revising and Refining the Theoretical Framework

Review the theoretical framework. Make sure that researchers have a clear understanding of its key concepts, assumptions, and relationships.

Revisit the research questions or objectives. Ensure they are well-defined and aligned with the theoretical framework.

Identify any weaknesses, gaps, or inconsistencies in the current theoretical framework. Look for areas where the theory might not adequately address the research questions.

Share the theoretical framework with peers and colleagues in the particular field. Ask for their advice and insights on how to improve it.

Consider whether alternative theoretical frameworks could better address the research questions. Explore other theories or models that might give a more appropriate foundation.

If the study has uncovered new concepts or variables that are not accounted for in the current framework, incorporate them as needed. Ensure they fit logically within the framework.

Revisit and refine the assumptions that underlie the theoretical framework. Ensure they align with the research objectives and reflect the current state of knowledge in the field.

Make sure that the theoretical framework aligns with empirical evidence and research findings in the field. Update it to reflect the latest research if necessary.

Check for internal consistency within the theoretical framework. Ensure that all concepts, relationships, and assumptions are logically connected and free from contradictions.

Define the variables and relationships within the framework. Use precise language to articulate how variables are linked and how they relate to the research questions.

Make sure that the citations and references within the theoretical framework are up-to-date and accurately represent the sources that inform the theory.

If researchers are unsure about certain aspects of the framework, consult with experts or scholars who specialize in the theoretical framework researchers are using. They can provide valuable insights.

Before finalizing the framework, consider pilot-testing it on a small scale to identify any practical challenges or issues that may arise during implementation.

Document any revisions or refinements made to the theoretical framework. This documentation will help to explain the evolution of the framework in the research report.

Once researchers have addressed any weaknesses or gaps and incorporated necessary revisions, finalize the theoretical framework. Ensure that it is well-structured, coherent, and logically sound.

Implement the revised theoretical framework in the research design, data collection, and data analysis. Ensure that the research methods align with the refined framework.

Throughout the research process, remain open to further revisions if new insights or data challenge the framework. Adapt and refine as needed to maintain alignment with the study.

4. Writing the Research Methodology

4.1 Introduction

The drive to inscription a perfect research methodology can be difficult, particularly if researchers are new to the process. Nevertheless, with this direction, researchers will gain the confidence and skills required to embark upon this critical aspect of the research study. By the end of this guide, researchers will have a clear roadmap for crafting a research methodology that not only meets the highest academic standards but also enhances the overall quality and impact of the research study. Whether researchers are conducting scientific experiments, surveys, case studies, or any other form of research, this guide will equip researchers to make the methodology section shine. This chapter guides how the research methodology should be presented.

4.2 Writing the Research Methodology

Start the methodology segment with a concise and clear overview of the research approach. Briefly describe the research design, methods, and techniques. This provides readers with a high-level understanding of what to expect.

Identify the research design (experimental, observational, qualitative, quantitative, case study, etc.). Justify the preference by explaining why it is the most appropriate for the research question.

Give detailed information about the participants or subjects in the study. Mention how it was selected, including any sampling methods used. Be specific about relevant demographics if related.

Express the data collection methods. Include details such as surveys, interviews, experiments, observations, or archival research. Explain why these methods were selected and how they align with the research objectives.

If researchers used specific instruments, tools, questionnaires, or materials, give information about them. Mention their sources, validity, and reliability if pertinent. Include any modifications or adaptations if made.

Describe the bit-by-bit processes for data collection. Be meticulous, so others can replicate the study. Mention any ethical considerations and approvals obtained if dealing with human subjects.

Point to the statistical or analytical techniques that are used to analyze the data. Explain why these methods were selected and how they relate to the research questions. Mention any software or tools used for analysis.

Thrash out the measures taken to ensure the reliability and validity of the data. This may include pilot testing, inter-rater reliability checks, or validation procedures for surveys/questionnaires.

If the study involves human subjects or sensitive data, explain the ethical considerations and approvals that are obtained. Discuss informed consent, confidentiality, and any potential risks to participants.

Admit the limitations of the research methodology. Address potential sources of bias, constraints, or shortcomings in the research approach.

Mention any challenges that encountered during the research process and how to mitigate them. This demonstrates the awareness of potential issues and the ability to adapt.

All over the methodology section, give justifications for every decision that is made. Explain why select certain methods, designs, and approaches over others. This demonstrates the thoughtfulness and rigor of the study.

Keep the methodology section well-organized, using subsections for different aspects (participants, data collection, or data analysis). Use clear and concise language, avoiding jargon or needless technical details.

If the methodology is based on established methods, theories, or models, cite the relevant literature to provide context and support for the preferences.

After writing the methodology section, review it carefully for clarity, coherence, and completeness. Seek advice from peers or mentors and make necessary revisions.

4.3 Writing the Research Philosophy

Before writing the research philosophy, make sure researchers have a clear understanding of the concept. Research philosophy means the set of beliefs, assumptions, and principles that support the research approach. Familiar research philosophies are positivism, interpretivism, and pragmatism.

Identify and choose the research philosophy that best suits the research question and objectives. Each philosophy has its own set of principles and assumptions, so select the one that aligns with the approach.

Introduce and explain the research philosophy researchers have selected. Give a concise definition and overview of the philosophy to provide readers with background.

Explain why researchers have selected this particular research philosophy for the study. Discuss how it aligns with the research objectives and the nature of the research question. Justify why it is the most appropriate approach.

Explore the assumptions associated with the selected philosophy. For example, if researchers selected positivism, mention the belief in an objective reality and the importance of empirical data. If researchers have selected interpretivism, highlight the emphasis on subjective understanding and multiple realities.

Connect the research philosophy with the overall research approach. Explain how the philosophy informs the choice of research design, data collection methods, and data analysis techniques. Show how the philosophy shapes the whole research process.

Admit any criticisms or limitations associated with the selected research philosophy. Be open about its constraints and how researchers plan to mitigate them in the study.

Epistemology deals with questions of knowledge and how it is acquired, while ontology pertains to the nature of reality. Discuss researchers' stance on these aspects within the context of the research philosophy. For example, if researchers are an interpretivist, researchers might embrace subjective knowledge (epistemology) and multiple realities (ontology).

Explain the implications of the research philosophy for data collection, analysis, and interpretation. Discuss how it might impact the reliability, validity, and generalizability of the research findings.

If the research philosophy is grounded in established philosophical or theoretical frameworks, cite relevant literature to give context and support for the preference.

Make sure that the explanation of the research philosophy is clear and concise. Avoid overly complex language or theoretical jargon that may confuse readers.

Demonstrate how the research philosophy integrates with other components of the research methodology, such as research design, data collection methods, and data analysis techniques. This ensures a cohesive and logical research framework.

4.4 Writing the Research Approach

State the type of common research approach. Common research approaches include quantitative, qualitative, mixed methods, case studies, experimental, survey, ethnographic, and more. Be clear about the approach that best suits the research question.

Present a concise summary of the selected research approach. Explain what it entails and why it is appropriate for the study.

Explain why this particular research approach. Discuss how it aligns with the research objectives, the nature of your research question, and the research philosophy. Justify why it is the most appropriate approach among alternatives.

Consider the key characteristics of the selected research approach. For example, if researchers are using a qualitative approach, mention that it focuses on in-depth understanding, uses non-numerical data, and often uses open-ended interviews or content analysis.

Describe the data collection methods associated with the research approach. Detail the tools, techniques, or instruments used for data gathering and justify why they are suitable for the study. Mention any modifications or adaptations there are.

Describe how to plan to analyze the data collected within the context of the research approach. Discuss the specific analytical techniques, software, or frameworks researchers will use.

Present the advantages and limitations of the selected research approach. Discuss the strengths and weaknesses as well as any constraints or challenges encountered during the research process.

Explain how the selected research approach is aligned with the research question and objectives. Show how it will help address the research problem and contribute to knowledge in the field.

Relate the research approach to the research philosophy (positivism, interpretivism, pragmatism). Explain how the approach embodies or aligns with the underlying philosophical stance.

Address any ethical considerations related to the research approach. Discuss issues such as informed consent, privacy, confidentiality, and participant rights, if related.

Show how the research approach integrates with other components of the research methodology, such as the research design and data collection and analysis methods. Ensure that there is logic and consistency in the approach.

Cite pertinent literature and studies that support the choice of research approach. This provides context and demonstrates that the approach is grounded in established methods and practices.

Keep the explanation of the research approach clear and concise. Use language that is accessible to a broad audience, avoiding unnecessary jargon.

After writing the research approach section, carefully proofread and revise it for lucidity, consistency, and completeness.

4.5 Writing the Research Design

Give a clear and concise title for the research design subsection. In the introductory paragraph, briefly explain the purpose of this section, which is to detail how the study was structured and conducted.

State the type of research design that was employed. Common research design types include experimental, correlational, descriptive, case study, longitudinal, cross-sectional, and more. Be specific about the design that best fits the research question.

Describe why this particular research design. Discuss how it aligns with the research objectives and the nature of the research question. Justify why it is the most appropriate design among alternatives.

Explain the setting or context in which the research took place. Mention if it was a field study, online environment, specific geographic location, or any other relevant context. Explain why this setting was selected and how it relates to the study.

Explain how data was collected, including any instruments or tools used. Be specific about the sequence of activities.

Explain the sampling methods employed to select participants or subjects. Discuss the rationale behind the sampling strategy, whether it's random sampling, purposive sampling, convenience sampling, or another method.

Explain the data analysis techniques and procedures that were used. Explain how the collected data was processed, organized, and analyzed. Mention any statistical tests, software, or frameworks used for analysis.

Discuss any ethical considerations related to the research design, such as informed consent, privacy, confidentiality, and participant rights. Explain how to adhere to ethical standards.

If the research design involves experimental or quasi-experimental methods, describe control measures that are implemented to minimize biases and extraneous variables.

Deal with how the research design ensured the validity and reliability of the study. Mention steps taken to enhance internal and external validity.

If using specific tools or instruments (surveys, questionnaires, interview guides), provide details about them. Discuss their development, validity, reliability, and any modifications there are.

Explain how the research design aligns with the chosen research philosophy (positivism, interpretivism, and pragmatism) and research approach (quantitative, qualitative, and mixed methods). Show how the design supports the overall research framework.

Explain how the research design fits within the broader context of the research methodology, including the research approach, data collection methods, and research philosophy. Ensure that there is consistency and lucidity across these components.

After writing the research design section, proofread it carefully for clarity, logic, and completeness.

4.6 Writing the Sample Design

Start with a clear title for the sample design part. In the introduction, briefly describe the purpose of this section, which is to describe the sample for the study.

Define the population or target group that the study aims to investigate. Specify the characteristics or criteria that define this population.

Explain the sampling method used to select the sample. Common sampling methods include random sampling, stratified sampling, convenience sampling, purposive sampling, and more. Explain why this particular method and how it aligns with the research objectives.

Indicate the size of the sample, which denotes the number of participants or subjects that are included. Justify the selected sample size, taking into consideration factors such as statistical power and resource constraints.

Describe the sampling frame, which is the list or source from which the sample. Describe how accessed or constructed the sampling frame and whether it accurately represents the target population.

Talk about potential sources of sampling bias and steps taken to minimize them. Explain how to ensure that the sample is representative of the population, considering factors such as non-response bias and selection bias.

Point to the procedures that were followed to select participants or subjects from the sampling frame. If relevant, discuss any randomization techniques or procedures used to ensure fairness.

If researchers encountered any constraints or challenges during the sampling process (difficulty in accessing certain groups), admit and discuss how it managed them.

Describe how the sample design is aligned with the research objectives and research question. Discuss how the sample represents the group that intends to generalize the findings.

Discuss any ethical considerations related to the sampling process, such as informed consent, privacy, and confidentiality. Explain how to adhere to ethical standards.

Explain how the sample design enhances the validity and generalizability of the findings. Discuss whether the sample is intended to be a representative cross-section, a specific subgroup, or a purposively selected group.

If relevant, give evidence of the adequacy of the sample in terms of statistical power. This may include calculations or references to power analyses.

Explain how the sample design aligns with the chosen research philosophy (positivism, interpretivism, and pragmatism) and research approach (quantitative, qualitative, and mixed methods). Show how the design supports the overall research framework.

Show how the sample design fits within the broader perspective of the research methodology, including the research approach, research design, data collection methods, and research philosophy. Ensure that there is consistency and lucidity across these components.

After writing the sample design section, proofread it carefully for clarity, lucidity, and completeness.

4.7 Selecting the Type of Data

Understand the fundamental differences between quantitative and qualitative data. Quantitative data involves numerical measurements, counts, and statistical analysis. It is used to quantify phenomena, establish patterns, and test hypotheses. Examples include survey responses, test scores, and numerical measurements. Qualitative data is non-numerical and is used to explore and understand complex phenomena in depth. It often involves textual or visual data, such as interviews, observations, focus group transcripts, and open-ended survey responses.

Articulate the objectives of the study. What are researchers trying to achieve with the study? Are researchers seeking to describe, explain, or explore a phenomenon? The research objectives will guide the choice of data type.

Formulate specific research questions that the study aims to answer. The research questions should align with the research objectives and help determine whether researchers need quantitative or qualitative data to address them.

Reflect on the nature of the phenomenon researchers are investigating. Is it something that can be easily quantified and measured or is it complex, context-dependent, and better understood through qualitative means?

Carry out a meticulous literature review to observe how similar studies have approached similar research questions. Pay attention to the data types used in these studies and the rationale behind their choices.

Think about the practical aspects of data collection. Assess whether it is feasible to collect the type of data that is needed given the available resources, time, and access to participants or sources.

In a few cases, it may be suitable to use both quantitative and qualitative data to gain a more comprehensive understanding of the research topic. This is known as a mixed methods approach and can provide a richer and more nuanced perspective.

Seek guidance from the research supervisors or experts in the field. They can provide valuable insights and help to make an informed decision about the type of data to collect.

If researchers are uncertain about the data type, consider conducting pilot testing using both quantitative and qualitative methods to assess which approach yields more valuable insights.

Consider the readers for the study. Consider whether the readers are more accustomed to quantitative or qualitative research and adapt the approach consequently.

Research is an iterative process and as researchers delve deeper into the study, researchers may find that the initial data type choice needs adjustment. Be open to reevaluating the approach as research progresses.

Alternative Method

If the study aims to quantify relationships, patterns, or trends and test hypotheses, quantitative data is typically more appropriate. Quantitative data involves numbers and statistical analysis, making it suitable for testing causal relationships and making. If the study aims to explore, describe, or understand complex phenomena, qualitative data is often preferred. Qualitative data provides rich, in-depth insights into the underlying processes, meanings, and experiences of participants.

Develop the research questions and think about whether they are best answered using quantitative or qualitative approaches. Quantitative research questions often start with "how many," "how much," "To what extent," or "what is the relationship between." They seek to establish numerical patterns and correlations. Qualitative research questions often begin with "how" or "why" and aim to uncover the experiences, perceptions, motivations, and meanings behind phenomena.

Consider the complexity of the topic that is being studied. Quantitative data is better suited for topics with clear variables and measurable outcomes. Qualitative data is valuable when dealing with complex or nuanced issues where the meaning and context matter. Quantitative data is typically collected from larger samples and allows for statistical generalization to a broader population. If researchers want to make general claims about a population, quantitative methods are more appropriate. Qualitative data is often collected from smaller samples and aims for in-depth understanding rather than generalizability. It provides insights into specific contexts and individuals' experiences.

Think about the data collection methods available for the study. Some methods are inherently quantitative (surveys, experiments), while others are qualitative (interviews, observations).

Evaluate the available resources. Quantitative research may require more resources for data collection and analysis, while qualitative research can be more resource-intensive in terms of data processing and interpretation.

Think about the research tradition or paradigm that aligns with the study. Some fields or research communities have a preference for quantitative or qualitative approaches, so it is essential to be aware of disciplinary norms.

In some cases, combining both quantitative and qualitative data (mixed methods) can provide a more comprehensive understanding of a research problem, especially when one type of data complements or validates the other.

Before finalizing the choice of data type, conduct a pilot study or preliminary research to assess the feasibility and suitability of the selected approach.

4.8 Selecting the Data Sources

Define the research question or objectives. This will guide the choice of data sources as they should be directly relevant to what researchers aim to investigate or analyze.

Based on the research question, think of possible data sources. These could include primary sources (data collected firsthand) or secondary sources (data collected by others).

If researchers are collecting primary data, researchers can design and distribute surveys or questionnaires to gather data directly from participants and conduct interviews (structured, semi-structured, or unstructured) with individuals or groups to collect qualitative data. Engage in systematic observations of events, behaviors, or phenomena. If relevant, design and conduct experiments to gather controlled data. If conducting qualitative research, engage in fieldwork to collect data through immersion in a specific context.

If researchers are using secondary data, access academic journals, books, and reports to review and cite existing studies and findings related to the research question. Use databases in a particular field to access relevant information. Explore archival materials, such as historical documents, records, or manuscripts, if applicable to the research. Collect data from online platforms, websites, or social media, but ensure data quality and reliability.

Irrespective of the source, critically assess the quality and reliability of the data. Consider factors such as credibility, relevance, accuracy, and currency. Ensure that the data aligns with the research objectives.

If researchers are collecting data, ensure that they follow ethical guidelines and obtain informed consent when necessary.

Give detailed descriptions of each data source that was used. How researchers collected the data for primary data sources, which the participants were, and any specific methodologies or instruments used. For secondary data sources, the name of the source, its origin, publication date, and relevance to the research.

Validate why researchers selected each data source. Explain how it aligns with the research objectives and contributes to the study. Discuss why it is the most appropriate source for the research.

Discuss the reliability and validity of the data sources. Explain any measures taken to ensure data quality and the steps researchers took to verify the accuracy of secondary data sources.

Cite the data sources properly, following the citation style (APA, MLA, Chicago) recommended by the journal.

Make sure that researchers provide enough information about the data sources to allow other researchers to replicate the study or assess the quality of the data.

Present information about the data sources in a concise and organized manner. Use subsections or headings to separate and describe each source.

4.9 Selecting the Data Collection Method

Think about the specific goals of the study. Are researchers trying to explore, describe, explain, or predict an occurrence? Adapt the data collection method to the objectives of the study. For instance, qualitative methods like interviews and focus groups are often employed for exploratory research, while quantitative methods like surveys are suitable for explanatory or predictive research.

Verify the type of data needed for the study. Is it quantitative (numeric) or qualitative (textual or categorical)? Quantitative data is often collected through surveys, experiments, or observations, while qualitative data is typically gathered through interviews, focus groups, or content analysis.

Think about the size and scope of the study. Larger-scale research may require quantitative methods that can efficiently collect data from a large sample, while smaller-scale studies might benefit from in-depth qualitative methods.

Measure the availability of existing data. Sometimes, secondary data sources, such as government databases or previously collected surveys, can be used to answer research questions, saving time and resources.

Evaluate the available resources. Some data collection methods, such as experiments, can be resource-intensive, while others, like online surveys, may be more cost-effective.

Think about the accessibility of the target population or participants. If the population is difficult to reach or involves sensitive issues, researchers may need to adapt the data collection method accordingly.

Make sure that the data collection method aligns with ethical principles. Obtain informed consent from participants, protect their privacy, and consider potential harm or discomfort associated with the method.

Assess the quality and validity of data that can be collected using the selected method. Some methods may produce more accurate and reliable data than others, depending on the research context.

The research design including whether it's cross-sectional or longitudinal, can influence the choice of data collection method. For instance, longitudinal studies may require repeated measures over time, which could affect the choice of method.

In some cases, using a combination of quantitative and qualitative methods (mixed methods) can provide a more comprehensive understanding of a research problem.

Before fully implementing your chosen method, consider conducting a pilot study to identify and address any issues or limitations in the data collection process.

4.10 Selecting the Variables

Define the research questions or objectives. What specific aspects of the research topic do researchers want to investigate or understand better?

Conduct a thorough literature review to identify key variables that have been studied about the research topic. This will help you understand what variables are relevant and have theoretical or empirical support.

Develop a conceptual framework or theoretical model that outlines the relationships between variables. This framework should guide the variable selection and help to identify the independent, dependent, and control variables.

Find out which variables are independent (predictors or causes) and which are dependent (outcomes or effects). Independent variables are the factors that are manipulated or studied to understand their impact on dependent variables.

Operationalise how researchers will measure or quantify each variable. Be specific about the measurement methods, units, and scales will use. Ensure that the operational definitions align with the research questions and objectives.

Depending on the research design and goals, consider including control variables. These are variables that can confound or influence the relationships between the independent and dependent variables. By including control variables, researchers can better segregate the effects of the independent variables.

Assess the feasibility of collecting data for each variable. Consider factors such as data accessibility, resources, and the time required to collect and analyze data for each variable.

Prioritize variables based on their relevance and significance to the research questions. Focus on variables that are most likely to provide meaningful insights and contribute to the research objectives.

While it is important to consider various variables, avoid overcomplicating the research design by including too many variables. A well-focused study with a manageable number of variables is often more effective.

Before finalizing the variable selection, consider conducting a pilot study or pre-testing the variables. This can help identify any issues with the operational definitions or measurement instruments.

In the research report, provide a clear rationale for selecting specific variables. Explain how they relate to the research questions and how their inclusion will contribute to the study's significance.

4.11 Selecting the Tools for Analysis

Think about the overall research design, such as whether it is experimental, observational, cross-sectional, longitudinal, or qualitative. Different research designs may need different statistical approaches.

Determine whether the data is quantitative (numeric) or qualitative (categorical or textual). Statistical tools are typically categorized into two main types: descriptive statistics for quantitative data and inferential statistics for making inferences from data.

The nature of the research questions plays a crucial role in selecting statistical tools. Ask yourself whether researchers are trying to describe data, test hypotheses, explore relationships, or make predictions. Descriptive statistics (mean, median, and standard deviation) are used to summarize and describe data. Inferential statistics, including t-tests, ANOVA, regression analysis, chi-square tests, and correlation analysis, are used to make inferences about populations based on sample data and to test hypotheses.

Consider the size of the sample. Some statistical tests are more appropriate for larger samples, while others are designed for smaller samples. Identify the types of variables in the study. Statistical tools vary based on whether researchers are analyzing continuous variables, categorical variables, ordinal variables, or a combination of these.

Be aware of the assumptions underlying different statistical tests. For instance, parametric tests like t-tests and ANOVA assume normality and homogeneity of variances, while non-parametric tests like the Mann-Whitney U test and Kruskal-Wallis test are more robust to violations of these assumptions.

Think about the research goals. If the primary aim is to explore relationships between variables, researchers may use correlation analysis or regression analysis. If researchers want to compare groups, ANOVA or chi-square tests may be appropriate.

The level of measurement of the variables (nominal, ordinal, interval, or ratio) will influence the choice of statistical methods. For example, nominal data may require chi-square tests, while interval or ratio data are amenable to parametric tests.

Make sure researchers have access to the necessary statistical software or tools to perform the selected analyses.

If researchers are unsure which statistical tools to use or how to interpret the results, consider consulting with a statistician or seeking guidance from a mentor with expertise in statistics.

Examine the distribution of the data. Depending on whether the data is normally distributed or not, researchers may need to select different statistical tests or consider transformations.

5. Writing the Empirical Results and Analysis

5.1 Introduction

The empirical results and analysis section of a research paper provides the foundation for drawing significant conclusions and insights from the collected data. This section changes raw data into precious knowledge, giving a widespread understanding of the research questions or hypotheses. Through careful examination and interpretation of empirical findings, researchers can expose patterns, trends, and associations within the dataset. This stage of the research process is crucial for substantiating or refuting the primary hypotheses, contributing to the existing body of knowledge, and informing future research directions. In this section, we explore the necessary task of presenting the empirical evidence, accompanied by a meticulous analysis that produces the implications and inferences of the study.

5.2 Steps of Presenting Empirical Results

Present the empirical results in a lucid and organized way. If there is quantitative data, use tables, graphs, and figures to enhance the visual representation of data, and for qualitative data, systematize themes, quotes, or main findings. Make sure that the results focus on the research objectives and are presented in a method that helps simple understanding.

Use suitable statistical techniques to analyze the data. Explain the statistical tests used and give pertinent measures of central tendency and variability. Give a short overview of the fundamental descriptive statistics of the data, for instance, means, standard deviations, and frequencies. This presents readers with an initial perceptive of the dataset before delving into more composite analyses. If relevant, thrash out the assumptions made in the statistical analyses and the rationale behind selecting an exacting method. Whether it is t-tests, ANOVA, regression, or other methods, describe why it was selected and make sure it aligns with the research questions or hypotheses. Exhibit the results in a clear and planned format. Employ tables and figures with useful titles and labels. Make sure that the presentation aligns with the directives.

Go beyond the raw data to interpret the findings. Accompany the tables and figures with textual understanding. Describe what the results mean in the context of the research questions. Consider the significance of each finding and highlight any patterns or trends that emerge from the data. Describe the sense behind the observed patterns and associations. Discuss whether the results support or contradict the initial hypotheses and if there are any unanticipated or counterintuitive findings. Put forward potential explanations for these outcomes and argue how they may impact the overall interpretation of the study.

Narrate the findings to existing literature. Emphasize similarities and differences between the results and those of earlier studies. This contextualization helps ascertain the contribution and uniqueness of the study to the broader academic discussion.

Admit the limitations of the study. Argue any constraints, biases, or methodological issues that might have influenced the results. This reveals a nuanced perceptive of the research background and supports a sensible interpretation of the findings.

Look at the practical implications of the results. Argue how the findings contribute to the field and how they can be applied in practical, theoretical, or real-world situations. Think about the broader impact and prospective avenues for future study on the findings. Endeavor for lucidity and succinctness in the writing. Present the information in a direct and reachable way, avoiding needless jargon. Employ lucid language to guide readers through the interpretation of the results.

5.3 Major Findings

Introduce the part where researchers will present the major findings. Give a short recap of the research questions or hypotheses to remind readers of the background.

Arrange the major findings under clear and descriptive headings. This helps readers navigate through the results section effortlessly. Each heading should signify an exact research question.

If relevant, start with descriptive statistics which gives a baseline understanding of the data before delving into more composite analyses.

Add the written presentation with tables, charts, and graphs. Visual images can often express complex information more capably. Make sure that visuals are suitably labeled and described in the text.

When presenting the findings, maintain an objective and realistic manner. Avoid interpretation at this stage; focus on reporting what the data reveals without injecting personal views.

Tackle each research question or hypothesis. Without a doubt state whether the findings support or reject each hypothesis. Be explicit in the language, avoiding unclear statements.

Make out and highlight any noteworthy patterns or trends in the data. This may entail pointing out significant differences, correlations, or other relationships. Employ succinct and clear language to explain these observations.

Where relevant, give numerical values to quantify the results. For example, if there's a significant difference between groups, state the effect size or percentage difference.

Argue the practical or theoretical significance of the findings. Why are these results significant and how do they contribute to the existing body of knowledge? Relate the findings to the broader context of the research area.

Draw links between the findings and existing literature. Discuss how the results focus or differ from earlier studies. This contextualization improves the scholarly significance of the study.

If there are unforeseen or contradictory findings, admit them. Present possible explanations or hypotheses for these outcomes. This demonstrates a nuanced perspective of the data.

Towards the end of the findings part, give a fusion that ties together the most important observations. Sum up the key takeaways without introducing new information.

If the findings are widespread, think about using subheadings to break down the results into convenient sections. This perks up readability and helps readers navigate through the information.

While summarizing findings for each research question, be aware of avoiding needless repetition. Undoubtedly state when findings are consistent across questions and only restate information when required for clarity.

5.4 Test of Hypotheses

Reintroduce the research question or questions and the corresponding hypotheses. Clearly state the null hypothesis (H0) and alternative hypothesis (H1) for each research question.

Indicate the statistical test or tests used for each hypothesis. Whether it is a t-test, ANOVA, regression, chi-square, or another method, give this information to bestow readers' context.

If the selected statistical test has assumptions, in brief mention whether those assumptions were met and if not, how researchers addressed any violations. Present the actual test statistics. Include the value of the test statistic, degrees of freedom, p-value, and significance level (alpha).

Coherent the decision rule. State the critical value or significance level and state whether researchers reject the null hypothesis if the p-value is less than this threshold or fail to reject if the p-value is more than this threshold. Be explicit and clear in the language.

If relevant to the statistical test, think about reporting an effect size measure. This gives additional information about the practical significance of the findings. For some tests, providing confidence intervals alongside point estimates can augment the interpretation. For example, in a regression analysis, report not only the coefficients but also the confidence intervals.

Interpret the results in the context of the research question. Discuss the implications of rejecting or failing to reject the null hypothesis. Explain the meaning of the statistical findings in simple language.

If the results are unexpected or contrary to the initial hypotheses, address this in the interpretation. Consider providing potential explanations or discussing the limitations that might have contributed to these results.

Relate the findings to existing literature. Discuss whether the results focus on or differ from earlier studies. This contextualization helps to establish the contribution of the study.

Admit any limitations in the study that may affect the interpretation of the results. This shows a thoughtful consideration of the research context and potential sources of error.

Think about the practical significance of the results. Even if a finding is statistically significant, its practical importance may vary. Argue how the results may be applied or what they mean in a broader context.

Conclude the section by summarizing the major outcomes of the statistical tests. Highlight the main findings that support or disprove the hypotheses. Use clear and short language. Avoid needless technical details, but make sure that the readers can understand the rationale, procedures, and outcomes of the hypothesis testing.

5.5 Policy Implications

Identify the policymakers or stakeholders who are likely to be interested in the study. Modify the language and recommendations to suit the needs and priorities of these readers.

Connect the research findings to specific policy objectives or goals. Display how the study addresses pressing issues or challenges pertinent to the policy context.

Emphasize the most important and actionable findings from the study. Focus on results that have direct significance to policymaking and can potentially lead to positive outcomes or improvements.

Review the context and background of the study to help policymakers understand the broader landscape. Coherent the problem or issue of research addresses and why it is related to policymaking.

If the findings suggest certain policies or interventions, discuss alternative approaches. Consider presenting a range of options and discuss the potential benefits and drawbacks of each. This demonstrates a nuanced perception of the complexities involved.

If feasible, enumerate the potential impact of the recommendations. Use statistics or estimates to help policymakers understand the scale of the issue and the potential benefits of implementing the suggested policies.

Thrash out the feasibility of implementing the proposed policies. Consider factors such as financial constraints, available resources, and potential challenges. Give insights into how these challenges can be mitigated. Conduct a basic cost-benefit analysis of the recommendations. Demonstrate how the benefits of implementing the suggested policies outweigh the potential costs, both in the short and long term.

Think about involving related stakeholders in the policymaking process. Discuss how engaging with various groups, including community members and experts, can contribute to the success of the proposed policies.

Deal with potential unintended consequences of the recommendations. Acknowledge any risks associated with the proposed policies and suggest strategies to monitor and mitigate these risks.

Outline the specific actions that policymakers can take based on the recommendations. Use actionable language and give guidelines on how to implement the proposed policies.

Thrash out the potential long-term impact of the recommendations. Demonstrate how implementing these policies can lead to sustained positive outcomes and contribute to the overall well-being of the community or society.

Consider the cultural and social context of the target population. Policies that focus on cultural norms and values are more likely to be accepted and successful. Present the policy implications clearly and concisely. Avoid jargon and technical language that may be unreachable to policymakers. Use simple language to increase understanding. External perspectives can help identify areas that need clarification and ensure that the recommendations are practical and realistic.

Strengthen the recommendations with evidence from the study. Reference the specific findings, data points, or examples to authenticate the effectiveness and importance of the suggested policies.

Articulate openness to further collaboration with policymakers. Offer the expertise and assistance in the implementation phase, emphasizing that the study is part of an ongoing discourse on the issue. Conclude the discussion on policy implications by summarizing the key points and reiterating the potential positive outcomes of implementing the recommendations.

5.6 Societal Implications

Identify the key findings of the study that have direct importance to society. Focus on results that have the potential to bring about positive changes or address societal challenges.

Join the research findings to larger societal issues or concerns. Explain how the study contributes to understanding or resolving these issues and why they matter on a societal level.

Allow and consider diverse perspectives within society. Discuss how the findings may impact different demographic groups, communities, or stakeholders. Be attentive to potential disparities or variations in societal impact.

Highlight the positive outcomes that may result from implementing the research findings in society. Discuss how the study has the potential to improve lives, address challenges, or contribute to positive social change.

Reveal the ethical implications of the study. Discuss how the findings may influence ethical considerations within society and ensure that the recommendations align with ethical standards.

Look at the relevance of the findings to policy development and implementation. Discuss how policymakers can use the study to inform or shape policies that address societal issues.

Think about the cultural context in which the research is situated. Discuss how cultural norms and values may influence the societal reception and application of the findings. Be responsive to cultural nuances.

Tackle potential unintended consequences of the findings on society. Recognize any risks associated with the application of the study and suggest strategies to monitor and mitigate these risks.

Think about how the findings may contribute to or detract from social equity. Discuss ways in which the study can promote fairness, justice, and inclusivity within society.

Advocate for community engagement and involvement in the application of the study. Discuss how communities can be active participants in utilizing the findings and share insights on their needs and preferences.

Search how the research can contribute to education and awareness within society. Discuss potential educational initiatives that can arise from the findings and how they can be disseminated to the public.

Outline the actionable steps that can be taken at the societal level based on the findings. Discuss how individuals, organizations, and communities can contribute to or benefit from the societal implications of the study.

Talk about the potential long-term impact of the findings on society. Consider how the positive outcomes may be sustained over time and how the study contributes to the overall well-being of individuals and communities.

Present the societal implications in a manner that is accessible to a broad audience. Avoid jargon and technical language and use clear and engaging language to enhance understanding among diverse stakeholders. External perspectives can help identify areas that need clarification and ensure that the recommendations are practical and inclusive. Conclude the discussion on societal implications by summarizing the key points and reiterating the potential positive outcomes of implementing the research findings at the societal level.

5.7 Suggestions and Recommendations

Summarize the major findings of the study. Give a short overview of the main outcomes that form the basis for the suggestions and recommendations.

State the purpose of the suggestions and recommendations. Make it apparent that the objective is to offer actionable advice that stems directly from the research findings.

Connect each recommendation to specific research questions or objectives. This helps readers understand the context and rationale behind each suggestion.

If there are multiple recommendations, prioritize them based on significance and feasibility. Begin with the most critical suggestions that directly address major research questions or gaps in the literature.

Whenever possible, quantify or qualify the recommendations. Give specific details on the suggested actions and this includes specificity and lucidity.

Thrash out alternative approaches or options. Recognize that different contexts may need different strategies and give insights into why the recommended approach is preferable.

Think about the feasibility of implementing the recommendations. Thrash out potential challenges and constraints as well as propose strategies for overcoming these obstacles.

Highlight the significance of involving appropriate stakeholders in the implementation of the recommendations. Argue how collaboration with key players can enhance the effectiveness of suggested actions.

Reveal the ethical considerations associated with the recommendations. Make sure that the proposed actions align with ethical standards and do not unintentionally cause harm.

Highlight the probable long-term impact of the recommendations. Thrash out how the suggested actions can contribute to sustained positive outcomes and address ongoing challenges.

Advocate for the establishment of mechanisms for monitoring and evaluating the implementation of the recommendations. Thrash out the importance of ongoing assessment to track progress.

Explain how collaboration among various stakeholders can improve the effectiveness of the recommendations. Promote the idea of working together to accomplish general goals.

Recognize the cultural context within which the recommendations will be implemented. Make sure that suggested actions are culturally sensitive and align with the values and norms of the target audience.

Outline the steps that need to be taken to implement each recommendation. Offer a roadmap or action plan that guides stakeholders through the process.

Present the recommendations clearly and concisely. Avoid unnecessary technical details, but ensure that the readers can understand the rationale and steps involved in implementing the suggestions. External viewpoints can help identify areas that need clarification and ensure that the recommendations are practical and realistic. Wrap up the argument on suggestions and recommendations by summarizing the major points and reiterating the potential positive outcomes of implementing the suggested actions.

5.8 Limitations of the Study

Acknowledge every study has limitations. Being honest and transparent about the constraints of the research enhances the credibility of the study.

Start the limitations section by introducing it in a clear and clear-cut way. Use a concise sentence to indicate that researchers are discussing the prospective shortcomings of the study.

Connect the limitations to the specific aspects of the research design. For example, thrash out limitations related to the sampling strategy, data collection methods, or analytical methods.

If relevant, thrash out any limitations related to the sample used in the study. This might include issues such as sample size, representativeness, or the generalizability of the findings to a broader population.

Explain any methodological limitations that may impact the validity and reliability of the results. This could involve issues with measurement tools, experimental design, or the control of extraneous variables.

Deal with limitations related to the data used in the study. Discuss any data collection challenges, missing data, or limitations in the availability and quality of the data.

Think about the external validity of the findings. Explain the extent to which the results can be generalized beyond the specific context of the study.

If the study involves the use of instruments or tools, thrash out any limitations associated with them. This could include the potential for measurement error or biases.

Recognize any potential biases introduced by participants. Discuss whether there are limitations related to the honesty, recall, or social desirability of participant responses.

Explain any limitations related to the time frame of the study. If time constraints affected the thoroughness of the investigation or the depth of the analysis, make that clear. Recognize limitations related to resources. This could include constraints in terms of funding, personnel, or access to specific tools or facilities.

If there were variables that were not under control during the study, discuss how these uncontrolled variables might impact the interpretation of the findings.

Give exact details about each limitation. The more concrete and detailed there are, the better readers will understand the potential impact of these limitations.

If appropriate, argue any efforts that were made to mitigate the impact of limitations. This could involve statistical corrections, sensitivity analyses, or other strategies to enhance the robustness of the findings.

While acknowledging limitations, avoid excessively insensitive self-criticism. Instead, focus on presenting limitations as natural constraints that are common in research. External perspectives can help ensure that adequately and appropriately addressed the limitations of the study. Wrap up the limitations by summarizing the major points and reiterating that these limitations do not reduce the overall value or significance of the study.

5.9 Scope for Future Research

State that the study addresses certain aspects; there are opportunities for additional research to build upon or extend the findings.

Explain how the study fits within the current state of the field. Emphasize the gaps or unanswered questions that the study identified, emphasizing the need for ongoing exploration.

Indicate specific questions or issues that the study did not fully address. Emphasize these as potential areas for future researchers to investigate and expand upon.

Think about alternative methodologies, perspectives, or approaches that could be explored in future research. Explain how different methodological choices might yield valuable insights.

If the study was limited to a specific sample or context, suggest how future research could expand these parameters. Explain the potential benefits of studying a more diverse sample or different settings.

If the study was cross-sectional, thrash out the potential for future research to use longitudinal designs. Longitudinal studies can provide insights into changes over time and causal relationships.

If different populations could be examined in future research. If the study focused on one age group, suggest investigating the same phenomena in other age groups.

If there are emerging trends or developments in the field, explain how future research could explore these areas. Think about how technological advancements or societal changes might impact the phenomena under study.

Recognize variables that were not thoroughly explored in the study and suggest that future research could delve deeper into these factors. This could include examining moderating or mediating variables.

Recommend comparative studies that could enhance understanding. Compare different interventions, groups, or contexts to identify nuanced differences or similarities that might inform practice or theory.

Look at the potential for cross-disciplinary research. Explain how insights from related fields could contribute to a more comprehensive understanding of the phenomena under investigation.

If there are advanced methodologies or analytical techniques that were not used in the study, suggest that future research explore these methods. Explain how they might enhance the precision or depth of investigation.

If the study has policy implications, explain how future research could focus on policy evaluation, implementation, or the development of new policies based on the findings.

If related, explain how future research could integrate technological advancements. This might include using new technologies for data collection, analysis, or intervention delivery.

If the study is original, support replication studies in different contexts or with different samples. Replication can help validate findings and assess their generalizability.

Give specific details about each suggested direction for future research. The more concrete and detailed they are, the more valuable the recommendations will be. Wrap up the section on the scope for future research by summarizing the major points and emphasizing the importance of ongoing inquiry to advance knowledge in the field.

5.10 Concluding remarks

Start the concluding remarks by summarizing the major findings of the study. Briefly remind the reader of the main outcomes and contributions of the study.

Revisit the research questions or objectives stated at the beginning of the study. Explain how the findings have addressed these questions or objectives and contributed to the existing body of knowledge.

Highlight the contributions of the study to the field. Explain how the study fills gaps in the literature, provides new insights, or advances understanding in a significant manner.

Reconnect with the overarching purpose of the study. Discuss how the study aimed to address a particular issue, solve a problem, or contribute to knowledge in a specific area.

Revisit the practical and theoretical implications of the findings. Discuss how the study has broader significance and how it might influence future research, practice, or policy.

Recognize the limitations of the study. Reveal the constraints and potential sources of error. Be honest and transparent about the scope and boundaries of the study.

Thrash out the methodological rigor of the study. Emphasize any steps taken to ensure the validity and reliability of the findings. This reinforces the credibility of the study.

Connect the findings to existing literature. Explain how the study aligns with or challenges earlier studies. This contextualization enhances the understanding of the study in the broader academic circumstance.

Admit any unanswered questions or areas for future research. This highlights the ongoing nature of inquiry in the field and gives potential directions for future researchers.

If the study introduces a novel concept, method, or approach, highlight its uniqueness. Discuss how the study adds something new and distinctive to the scholarly conversation.

If relevant, articulate gratitude to those who contributed to the research. This might include colleagues, mentors, participants, or funding agencies. Admit the collaborative effort that went into the study.

Thrash out the practical applications of the findings. If the study has implications for real-world practices or interventions, highlight how these can be applied to benefit individuals, organizations, or communities.

Reflect on the broader social impact of the study. Discuss how the findings might contribute to positive social change, deal with societal challenges, or enlighten public discourse.

Conclude the remarks with a strong and memorable statement. Sum up the overarching message that wants readers to take away from the study. This could be a call to action, a reflection on the significance of the topic, or a forward-looking statement.

Maintain the tone of the concluding remarks positive and forward-looking. Even if the study uncovered challenges or limitations, focus on the opportunities for growth, development, or further investigation.

Maintain the concluding remarks concise and focused. Avoid introducing new information in this section and strive for lucidity and succinctness. Make sure that the message is lucid, logical, and effectively captures the spirit of the study.

Glossary

Analysis: The systematic examination and interpretation of data to uncover patterns, relationships, and insights relevant to the research question.

Citation: A reference to a source of information, typically included in scholarly documents to acknowledge the contributions of others and provide credibility to the research.

Collaboration: Working together with others, often across disciplines or institutions, to enhance the quality and impact of research outcomes.

Data Collection: The process of gathering relevant information or evidence through various methods such as surveys, experiments, interviews, or observations.

Data: Facts, figures, or information collected, analyzed, and interpreted in the context of a research study.

Dissemination: The distribution and communication of research findings to relevant stakeholders, including academic peers, practitioners, policymakers, and the public.

Ethics: Principles and standards of conduct governing research practices, including issues such as informed consent, confidentiality, and avoidance of harm to participants.

Hypothesis: A testable statement or prediction about the relationship between variables, often formulated based on theory or previous research.

Impact: The influence, significance, or effect of research on knowledge, policy, practice, or society at large.

Literature Review: A critical analysis and synthesis of existing research and scholarship relevant to a particular topic or research question.

Methodology: The systematic, theoretical analysis of the methods applied in a particular field of study.

Peer Review: The process by which scholarly work is evaluated by experts in the same field to assess its quality, validity, and contribution to knowledge.

Quality Research: Research characterized by rigor, validity, reliability, ethical conduct, and meaningful impact.

Quality: The degree to which research meets predefined standards of excellence, rigor, and relevance.

Reliability: The consistency and stability of research findings, indicating the degree to which results can be replicated or trusted.

Research: Systematic investigation or inquiry aimed at discovering, interpreting, or revising facts, theories, applications, and phenomena.

Sampling: The selection of a subset of individuals or items from a larger population, intended to represent the population as a whole.

Validity: The extent to which a research study accurately measures or reflects the concept or phenomenon it claims to measure or reflect.

Epilogue

As I conclude this journey through the labyrinth of research, I am reminded of the winding paths, dead ends, and unexpected discoveries that marked the way. The pursuit of quality research is not merely a quest for knowledge but a testament to perseverance, curiosity, and the relentless pursuit of truth.

In the course of writing this book, I have encountered countless individuals who share a passion for inquiry and a dedication to excellence. Their stories have inspired me, their insights have challenged me, and their collaboration has enriched the fabric of this work.

Yet, for all the wisdom gleaned from the experiences of others, there is no substitute for personal engagement with the subject matter. Research, at its core, is a deeply personal endeavor—a journey of self-discovery as much as it is a quest for understanding.

As we part ways, dear reader, I urge you to embrace the challenges that lie ahead with courage and conviction. Approach each new inquiry not as an obstacle to be overcome but as an opportunity to grow, to learn, and to make a meaningful contribution to the world of knowledge.

Remember, the pursuit of quality research is not a destination but a journey—a journey that begins anew with each question asked, each hypothesis tested, and each discovery made.

May your path be illuminated by the light of curiosity, guided by the compass of critical thinking, and enriched by the diversity of perspectives that surround you.

Farewell, and may your quest for quality research be as rewarding as it is endless.

With warm regards,

[AMALENDU BHUNIA]

References

Booth, W. C., Colomb, G. G., & Williams, J. M. (2008). The Craft of Research. University of Chicago Press.

Creswell, J. W. (2014). Research Design: Qualitative, Quantitative, and Mixed Methods Approaches. Sage Publications.

Denzin, N. K., & Lincoln, Y. S. (Eds.). (2018). The Sage handbook of qualitative research. Sage Publications.

Gall, M. D., Gall, J. P., & Borg, W. R. (2007). Educational research: An introduction. Pearson.

Gravetter, F. J., & Forzano, L. B. (2018). Research methods for the behavioral sciences. Cengage Learning.

Greenhalgh, T. (2019). How to Read a Paper: The Basics of Evidence-Based Medicine and Healthcare. John Wiley & Sons.

Hart, C. (2018). Doing a Literature Review: Releasing the Social Science Research Imagination. Sage Publications.

Maxwell, J. A. (2012). Qualitative research design: An interactive approach. Sage Publications.

Mertens, D. M. (2014). Research and Evaluation in Education and Psychology: Integrating Diversity with Quantitative, Qualitative, and Mixed Methods. Sage Publications.

Neuman, W. L. (2013). Social research methods: Qualitative and quantitative approaches. Pearson Education.

Silverman, D. (2016). Qualitative Research. Sage Publications.

Swales, J. M., & Feak, C. B. (2012). Academic Writing for Graduate Students: Essential Tasks and Skills. University of Michigan Press.

Trochim, W. M., & Donnelly, J. P. (2008). The research methods knowledge base (3rd ed.). Atomic Dog.

Turabian, K. L., Booth, W. C., Colomb, G. G., Williams, J. M., & Bizup, J. (2018). A Manual for Writers of Research Papers, Theses, and Dissertations: Chicago Style for Students and Researchers. University of Chicago Press.

Yin, R. K. (2017). Case study research and applications: Design and methods. Sage Publications.